THE ART OF

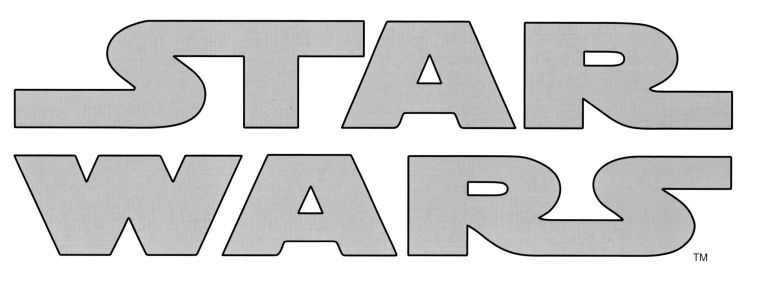

EPISODE I

THE PHANTOM MENACE™

This book is dedicated to Rick McCallum,
George Lucas, Doug Chiang, Gavin Bocquet,
&
the Star Wars Art Department.

SPECIAL THANKS TO

THE BRESMAN AND LEE FAMILIES

Roberta Cairney
David Craig
David Gordon
Mark Mrnka
Meredith Wolf Schizer
Mary Wu
Pat York

BALLANTINE BOOKS
Senior editor: Steve Saffel
Director of production: Frederic L. Dodnick
Associate managing editor: Alexandra E. Krijgsman
Director of contract administration: Amelia Zalcman

LUCAS LICENSING
Vice president, licensing: Howard Roffman
Director of publishing: Lucy Autrey Wilson
Continuity editor: Allan Kausch
Publishing art editor: Iain Morris

LUCASFILM LTD.

Troy Alders, Matt Azeveda, Michael Blanchard, Mark Becker, Ben Burtt, Scott Carter, Jenny Craik, Jo Donaldson, Cheryl Edwards, Kathryn Farrar, Maureen Forster, Tom Forster, Steve Gawley, Greg Gawlowski, Michael Giesbrecht, Justin Graham, Joel Grande, Robin Gurland, Lynne Hale, Industrial Light & Magic, JAK Films and the Leavesden Crew, Ardees Jundis, Halina Krukowski, Nicole Love, Aaron Lubarsky, Paul Matwiy, Rick McCallum, Tina Mills, Janet Nielsen, David West Reynolds, Roel Robles, Jett Sally, Steve Sansweet, Darlene Sattel, Jon Shenk, Martin Smith, Blake Tucker, Jim Ward, Pooneh Zandazma, and, of course, George Lucas

THE ART OF

STAR WARS™

EPISODE I

THE PHANTOM MENACE™

WRITTEN BY JONATHAN BRESMAN

LUCAS BOOKS

EBURY PRESS
LONDON

Ebury Press
Random House
20 Vauxhall Bridge Road, London SW1V 2SA

The Random House Group. Limited Reg. No. 954009

A CIP catalogue record for this book is available from the British Library

www.starwars.com
www.randomhouse.co.uk

ISBN 0 09 186870 X

Edited by Allan Kausch (Lucasfilm) and Steve Saffel (Del Rey)
Photography by Jonathan Fisher, Maureen Forster, Tom Forster, Greg Gawlowski, Keith Hamshere,
Alexander Ivanov, Giles Keyte, Ellen Lee, David Owen

Designed by Ellen Lee

Printed and bound in Germany by Mohndruck, GmbH

Papers used by Ebury Press are natural, recyclable products made from wood grown in sustainable forests.

FURTHER EPISODE I TITLES FROM RANDOM HOUSE

STAR WARS: EPISODE I
THE PHANTOM MENACE
ILLUSTRATED SCREENPLAY
GEORGE LUCAS 0091868688 £9.99 PAPERBACK

STAR WARS: EPISODE I
THE MAKING OF THE PHANTOM MENACE
LAURENT BOUZEREAU AND JODY DUNCAN 009186867x £14.99 PAPERBACK

STAR WARS: EPISODE I
THE PHANTOM MENACE
THE FACSIMILE EDITION SCRIPT BOOK
GEORGE LUCAS 0091868726 £14.99 PAPERBACK
FEBRUARY 2000

C-3PO TALES OF THE GOLDEN DROID
JOSH LING AND DANIEL WALLACE 0091873576 £60 BOXED SET
OCTOBER 1999

Preface

In 1977, George Lucas, a director primarily known for *American Graffiti*, a nostalgic film about early '60s small-town California teenagers, stunned audiences with the release of *Star Wars: A New Hope*. A fusion of fable, fairy tale, and classic movie serial, Lucas had created a universe remarkable for both its epic scope and meticulous detail.

While moviegoers the world over marveled at what Lucas had wrought, George himself remained somewhat unsatisfied with the results, yearning for a palette far beyond the capabilities of 1970s special-effects technology. That remained the case for two decades—it wasn't until the 1997 release of the digitally-enhanced *Star Wars Trilogy Special Edition* that the state of the art finally advanced to the point where Lucas could construct a cosmos without having to compromise. And so, fully-armed, he set to work on *Star Wars: Episode I The Phantom Menace*.

Lucas began by searching for a team of conceptual designers who could develop every last corner of the *Star Wars* universe. Expanding on the work of such greats as Ralph McQuarrie and Joe Johnston, a new generation of artists would envision new worlds, new characters, and new societies.

However, universe building can be a grueling process. As the process began, each element existed only in the mind's eye—in this case, the mind of George Lucas. So each artist knew he might be called upon for more than expertise with pen and paper. He or she might be asked to become an interstellar anthropologist, zoologist, or engineer, an expert in imaginary cultures, customs, and architecture.

Thus, it became the lot of the conceptual artist to figure out what the director would want, perhaps even before the director necessarily knew he wanted it. The director, in turn, would review each and every rendering, making alterations and asking for revisions, guiding the evolution of his universe.

This conceptual evolution normally takes place after the script has been finished but before the filming has begun, so the director can amass all the raw materials he will need to give his characters form, and to place them in a context through which they will spring to life. On Episode I, however, much of the conceptual artwork was created in concert with the storytelling, and it continued to evolve throughout the production of the film. Because computer graphics technology allowed him to create and explore new photorealistic effects, Lucas could continue to tweak his ideas and modify the look of the film the entire time—even after he had finished principal photography.

As a result, every aspect of Episode I has a finely crafted look to it. Led by design director Doug Chiang, and production designer Gavin Bocquet, dozens of artists continuously visualized and polished the film's look over the course of four years—a nearly unprecedented amount of time to have an art department working on one film.

This book offers an in-depth look at the lengths to which the art department went in its construction of George Lucas' universe. The evolutionary stages for each major character, vehicle, and planet are displayed, so that the reader can get a sense of how the film was painstakingly sculpted, and, finally, how a new style of filmmaking was founded.

Jonathan Bresman

Jonathan Bresman
San Francisco
May 1999

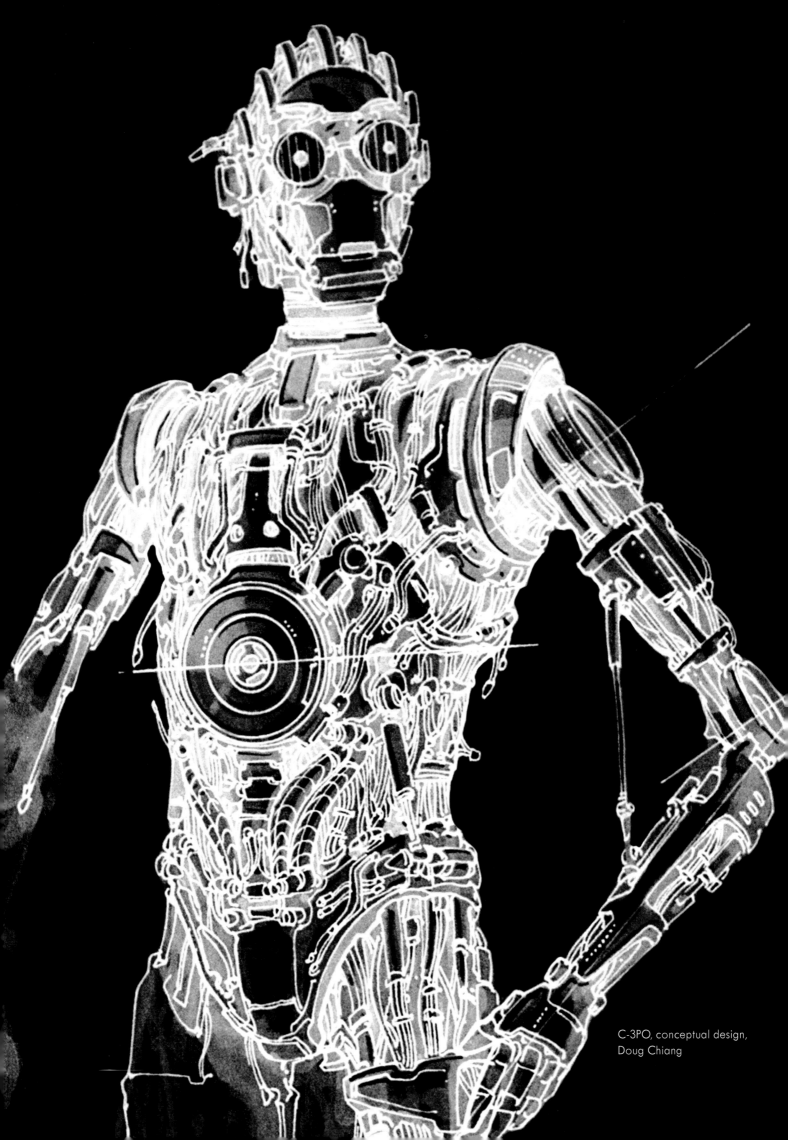

C-3PO, conceptual design,
Doug Chiang

TABLE OF CONTENTS

Foreword

During the autumn of 1994, George Lucas announced that he was writing Episode I and was staffing up an art department for the first of three new prequels. For many designers and artists who grew up as the *Star Wars* generation, myself included, it was the opportunity of a lifetime.

The news spread rapidly, and soon hundreds of portfolios were submitted for consideration. By January of 1995, the art department was formed and the daunting task of translating George's vision began. The Episode I art department grew from a small staff of two, myself and Terryl Whitlatch, to as many as seventeen during our peak. Our talents varied as much as our individual personalities. Some of us were passionate creature experts, while others focused on costume design, and still others on hardware. It was my responsibility to supervise and channel this diversity of creative energy in a cohesive direction so as to fulfill George's vision.

It was my pleasure to work with some of the most talented artists in the industry in an environment filled with energy and inspiration. For me, it was like attending the best art and film school one can imagine, with George as our mentor. We fueled each other's creativity as ideas jumped from one drawing board to another to combine and grow.

For more than three years following, the art department and I designed everything from battleships to belt buckles to buildings. We adhered to George's design philosophy of combining, in unusual ways, seemingly unrelated concepts to create striking forms. Thousands of sketches, models, and paintings were developed as we tried to create the world of Episode I. In order to create a future, we looked into the past, and drew inspiration from history and nature in order to give our fictional creations a realistic foundation.

We strove to create designs that would elicit intellectual as well as emotional responses. Certain forms convey aggression, while others invite comfort. Imbuing our works with these traits enhances their effectiveness. The MTT troop transport vehicle, for instance, was designed to subliminally resemble a charging bull elephant. Although not immediately recognizable, these elephant features, on a subconscious level, reinforce the MTT's fearsome quality.

At times, when we struggled with challenges that seemed too daunting to overcome, the clarity of George's vision always guided us. George had an uncanny ability to strengthen a design by modifying or adding an element. We struggled, for example, to find Sebulba's ideal Podracer engine configuration. After trying various orientations, I presented to George our two best options and asked which solution was better. George chose neither. Instead, he took the model and aligned the engine cowlings into an "x" shape. This new configuration transformed the meek engine into an aggressive, sleek configuration more fitting of the champion's personality. It was the perfect answer—and typical of George's clarity.

George taught us many things about successful film design. Design needs to be more than just beautiful art. In addition to being aesthetically pleasing, it needs functionality. And foremost, the design needs to support the story rather than detract from it. In every instance, we sought to determine whether a design was successful, while at the same time determining whether or not it was appropriate to the story. This was one of our main challenges in designing Episode I, where most aspects of the film's reality needed to be conceived and created from scratch.

What you see in this book are examples of our focused experimentation. You will see the development of ideas, how sketches combine and evolve with others into the final concepts. As we designed, we never lost sight of our goal—to create a look distinct from, yet consistent with, the original *Star Wars* trilogy. The artistry of the previous *Star Wars* artists and designers set the standard for us, and we hope these images share with you some of our joy in designing for Episode I.

D.CHIANG

Doug Chiang
Skywalker Ranch
May 1999

Introduction

In early 1995, one of the more unusual pre-production teams in the annals of modern cinema began meeting in the attic of Skywalker Ranch's main house in Marin County, CA. They had been assembled to design a new *Star Wars* movie—a movie that would live up to and be consistent with the original films, without being overshadowed by them. Although understandably nervous, and more than a little bit intimidated by the enormity of their task, this new team of artists happily converted the sunny, skylit attic into a functioning art department.

Acrylic paints were purchased for creating moody, evocative production paintings. Markers of every imaginable color were collected so that the designers might render concept sketches in a dazzling array of hues and tones. Entire arsenals of pencils were requisitioned so that thousands of storyboards could be sketched. Sheet upon sheet of foam core was procured for the building of architectural models. Claylike substances such as Sculpey or resin were acquired for creature-sculpting, and high-powered computers with the latest in speedy microprocessors were bought for the generation of digital simulations. Once this preparatory work was complete, and all the necessary tools were gathered, the artists sat back and eagerly awaited their marching orders.

The artists soon discovered—much to their surprise—that director George Lucas hadn't yet completed the script. And rather than "marching orders," what he gave them was a bizarre and exotic list of items: Otoh Gunga, the Podrace, Neimoidians, and so on. At first, Lucas didn't spell out exactly what these things were, nor what he expected them to look like. He did, however, clearly convey a general design philosophy: feel free to create.

While the artists couldn't quite believe they were being given such carte blanche, Lucas knew exactly what he was doing. He had studied the work of many different designers, and had chosen his team from those who were able to temper their fantastic designs with a dose of real world functionality. This idea is at the heart of the *Star Wars* style—everything has to look like it has a history, and might actually be used, worn, wielded, driven, or flown. Lucas knew that his team innately understood this, and so he wasn't afraid to give them their freedom.

Traditionally, a movie art department will be established after the screenplay has been completed. George Lucas, however, felt that too many science fiction and fantasy films focus on the visuals, without paying enough attention to the story, and he decided to join the two processes together organically, so each might gain strength from the other. As a result, design work began even as Lucas fleshed out his outline. He would come in each Friday with new story ideas, from which the artists worked to match his mental picture.

None of the artists had ever collaborated so closely with a director before. Generally, there is little back-and-forth communication between artist and director. Sometimes a director will send very explicit notes as to what he wants, while other times he will leave the artists to their own devices.

Lucas wanted his team to think, and think big. A mode of operation developed where the artists would offer him multiple renditions for each of his ideas. He would literally stamp each of the alternatives with red-inked rubber stamps reading "FABULOUSO," "OK," or—in the case of rejection—"DEEP REGRET." He would then return the chosen image to the artist, who would create additional variations. This evolutionary process would continue indefinitely as the artists covered the walls

Writer/director George Lucas

Skywalker Ranch

Skywalker Ranch's main house

The Star Wars *art department in front of the main house*

Design director Doug Chiang, George Lucas, and concept designer Iain McCaig

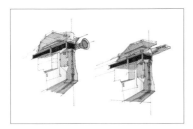

The Republic Cruiser Radiant VII, *conceptual design, Doug Chiang*

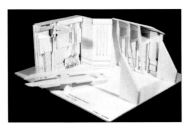

Trade Federation Battleship hangar bay, foam core model, Ellen Lee

STAPs versus air whales, production painting, Doug Chiang

Jar Jar and Qui-Gon in the swamp, storyboard, Iain McCaig

Jar Jar and Qui-Gon in the swamp, videomatic with animatic background, Ben Burtt/concept design department

Trade Federation invading Theed, animatic, Kevin Baillie

with their work, until finally a design would leap out and strike Lucas as having just the right look to it. Then, and only then, was a sketch allowed to move on to the next phase: modeling.

A sketch is two-dimensional. Just because something looks great on paper doesn't mean it will work in the real world. So sketches of sets, creatures, and vehicles became models and maquettes made of foam, card, plastic, Sculpey, or resin. This enabled Lucas to hold these models in his hands, get a feel for them, and—if necessary—call for still further modifications.

More often than not, the physical models were turned into computer simulations. Once a creature or vehicle design passed the modeling test, rough computer models were developed and animated, to get a sense of how they might move. At this stage, if the original designs proved in any way impractical, they could be reviewed and tweaked as needed.

When all this had been satisfactorily completed, the final design work was sent off to the production team. Sets were built, costumes sewn, masks were molded, ships were built, and so on to prepare for principal photography. If the work was to be purely digital, the designs went to ILM—Industrial Light & Magic.

As the designs started to solidify and the screenplay came together, design director Doug Chiang generated a series of production paintings to represent key moments in the story. These provided the artists and the director with an opportunity to bring all the elements of a particular sequence together in context, to get a sense for the mood, composition, lighting, action, and overall design. Essentially, they conveyed the overall texture and feel of the film, and were used to bridge the gap between the design and story processes.

To further bridge this gap, Lucas broke down the story into sequences so the artists could begin storyboarding. Storyboards look a bit like comic strips—each panel conveys a moment in time. Storyboards are also employed to communicate camera angle and movement, character action and scene composition.

Movies are about motion, though, and traditionally, storyboards are static by nature. It became critical to evoke a sense of action for many elements of the story, whether implying camera movement, fight choreography, or vehicular motion. In the past, moviemakers sometimes relied on rough mini-cartoons known as pencil tests, or on filmed sequences of storyboards, called story reels. For Episode I, Lucas took traditional techniques to the next level of sophistication, and had videomatic and animatic sequences created for many of the scenes.

Animatics and videomatics are mini-movies that give the director a sense of a scene's timing and pacing. They also help to establish the proper kind of camera lens and lighting that will be used. Videomatics are rough drafts of scenes involving human actors, shot on video tape with random crew members acting out the parts of the characters, and will sometimes have stock footage cut in to represent the effects shots. For example, World War II aerial combat scenes might be employed to represent space battles. The videomatics are then used on set as reference for the "real" actors, and function as placeholders until the finished footage can be cut in.

Modern animatics are computer-generated rough drafts of scenes that will require special effects work, such as Episode I's Podrace or the end battle, and they will replace the stock footage of the videomatic. Animatics are often composited with live-action footage, and may remain in the cut until they are replaced by their finished, photorealistic counterparts. The animatics and videomatics acted as templates for the final cut, allowing Lucas to create a preliminary version of the film well before production began. Once they were finished, they, too, were handed over to the production team, along with the storyboards and designs that would be used for live-action filming.

On most films an artist's responsibilities are fulfilled once designs have been turned over to the production team. This wasn't the case on Episode I.

Lucas knew he was going to want to tweak a lot of the live-action sets in post-production. He also realized that he wouldn't know just how far he would want to go with these enhancements until he was physically on set. So he made the unusual decision to keep his art department working throughout the duration of filming and post-production.

For Lucas' nonlinear approach to digital filmmaking, the physical incarnation of a design simply became one more draft. Each full-size set would give Lucas a chance to walk around and play with camera angles, and if he felt that the design of the set could still be improved upon, then footage of the set would be sent back to the art department for modification. For example, Lucas decided that the walls of the Jedi Council Room were too high, and didn't allow for interesting composition. But this didn't stop him from shooting the scenes he needed. He simply sent the completed footage back to the art department, which redesigned the set around the actors. The art department, in turn, sent the changes to ILM. Then ILM produced the final, film-quality execution via digital enhancement.

The Theed Palace footage, shot at the ornate Italian palace known as the Palazzo Reale, went through a similar process. Lucas wanted to increase the scale of the already impressive palace, so the art department was assigned the task of taking existing footage and punching out walls, adding in nonexistent windows, expanding hallways, doubling the heights of ceilings, and so on.

In the case of the Podrace hangar, it was built in a certain configuration and following a certain scale, but after Lucas edited the scene together, he decided it wasn't big enough. So the hangar went through an entire redesign which involved painting out a great deal of the set and enhancing it as a huge miniature.

Design and redesign took place constantly during the making of Episode I, leading to a method of filmmaking in which the process continued, even after the camera began rolling. Buildings were rebuilt, landscapes altered, and imperfections eliminated.

This book is filled with such "fixes." The result is a film that is finished to an extraordinarily fine degree. Looking back, the development of a costume, character, or spaceship from start to finish may seem straightforward. However, for each work that gets the stamp of approval there are frequently many, many versions that have been cut—each rendered with just as much care and craftsmanship as the ones that have been approved. It is through this constant editing that the look of the film evolved, along with the story.

Here, in a sense, is the evolutionary record of Episode I—the unseen art that served as the foundation of the film. George Lucas and producer Rick McCallum didn't commission the works in this volume so they would be put on display. The art department created these extraordinary models and illustrations simply to serve as tools that would further the exploration and evolution of the *Star Wars* universe. As the artwork will demonstrate, it was an exploration infused with a sense of excitement and energy from concept to completion.

Lucas and producer Rick McCallum (second from right) consult with the concept design team

Starfighter droid and battle droid in Trade Federation battleship hangar, animatic frame, Jeff Wozniak

Theed palace, storyboard, designed around live action footage, Kurt Kaufman

Theed palace and cityscape, animatic frame, Ryan Tudhope

Podrace hangar interior, animatic frame, Alex Lindsay

The Star Wars art department

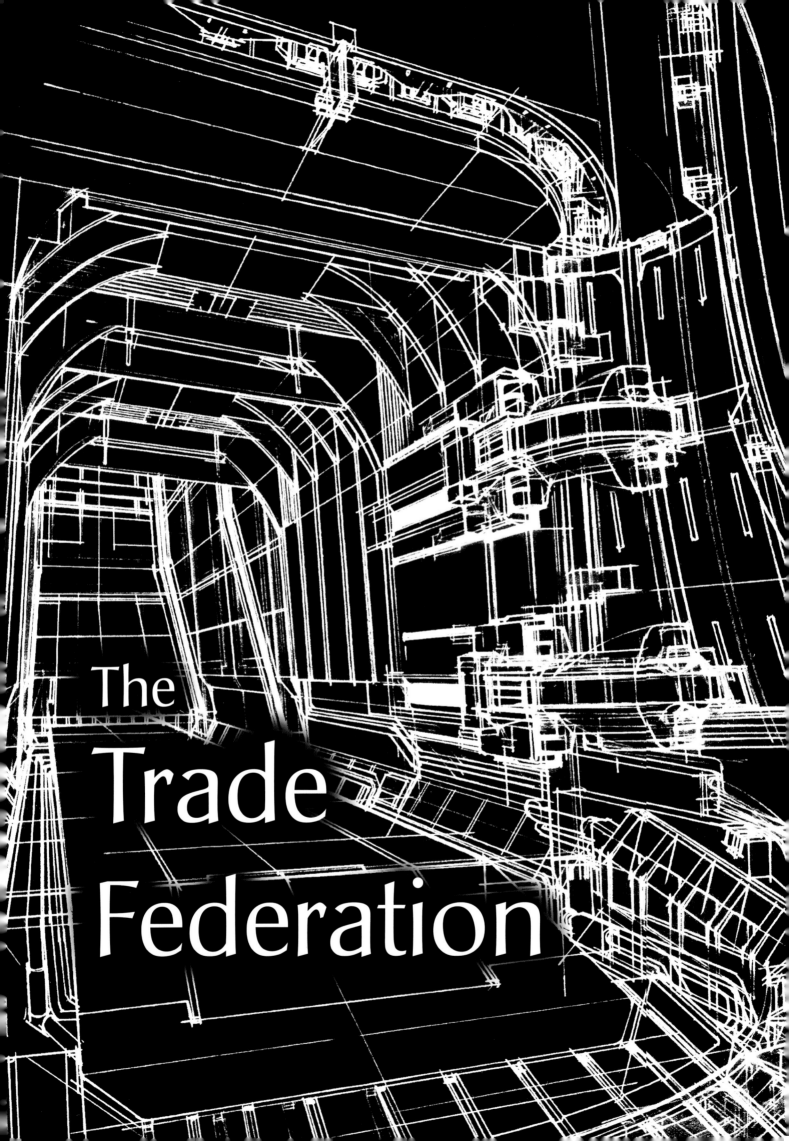

The Trade Federation

History is rife with instances wherein moneyed interests impact the political status quo. An extreme example was the overthrow of Queen Liliuokalani of Hawaii. In the 1890s, a group of businessmen, ignoring the orders of President Grover Cleveland, forced the Queen to abdicate her throne. They replaced the government with one that would be more sympathetic to their interests.

In *The Phantom Menace*, the Trade Federation—a corporate army of licensed pirates—attempts their own assault on Queen Amidala of the planet Naboo. They hope to force the Queen to surrender her authority, so the Trade Federation can gain control of the Galactic Trade routes. This would increase its fortune immeasurably.

The Neimoidian leaders of the Trade Federation are avarice personified. They roam the galaxy, constantly accumulating wealth, spacecraft, and weaponry, and thus have built a massive, interstellar fleet. Led by the evil Viceroy Nute Gunray, the Neimoidians pledge no allegiance to any particular planet or governing body, and seem content to connive from the cold expanse of space. Their sense of greed is so strong that it compels them to form an alliance with the Force-wielding Sith, despite the obvious danger such a partnership would entail. A spoiled, cowardly lot, the Neimoidans generally employ droids to conduct the physical aspects of their skullduggery, to avoid getting their hands dirty. Because the Neimoidians eschew all physical activity, George Lucas specified that their bodies should appear weak and frail, their muscles atrophied. The result would be rich, repellent old beings who rely on their silent, mindless, robotic work force to meet their every physical need, leaving them free to conspire and scheme. And as a mirror for their propensity to spin webs of deceit, the Neimoidians would exhibit a somewhat shriveled, spidery appearance. Aspects of this appearance would extend to their technology, as well—for example, Nute Gunray's walking chair.

Their landing fleet was designed to display a predatory, animalistic look, and so the ships are based on lions, elephants, and dragonflies. As for the Neimoidian battleships, they are a testament to the treachery of the Trade Federation. Built to look like innocent freighters, they are actually heavily armed, and contain entire concealed armies of battle droids.

Neimodian clothing has a rich, decadent look to it. Based on kabuki costumes, their robes and crowns look like some *nouveaux riches* attempt to bestow upon themselves the trappings of nobility. Underneath it all, however, the Neimoidians would prove to be wretched, grotesque weaklings who rely entirely too much on their technology.

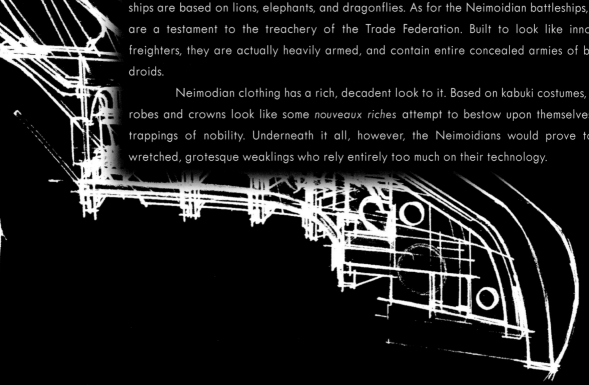

1

The Republic Cruiser, Radiant VII, approaching the Trade Federation battleship, initial and final production paintings
1, 2 Doug Chiang

In the opening shot of the film, the Trade Federation battleship, disguised as a freighter, looms menacingly over the peaceful world of Naboo. Chiang gave these ships their intricately rendered surfaces by using acrylics, which allow for fine detail work.

Pages 4–5: Trade Federation landing ship cargo hold/hangar bay, conceptual design
Jay Shuster

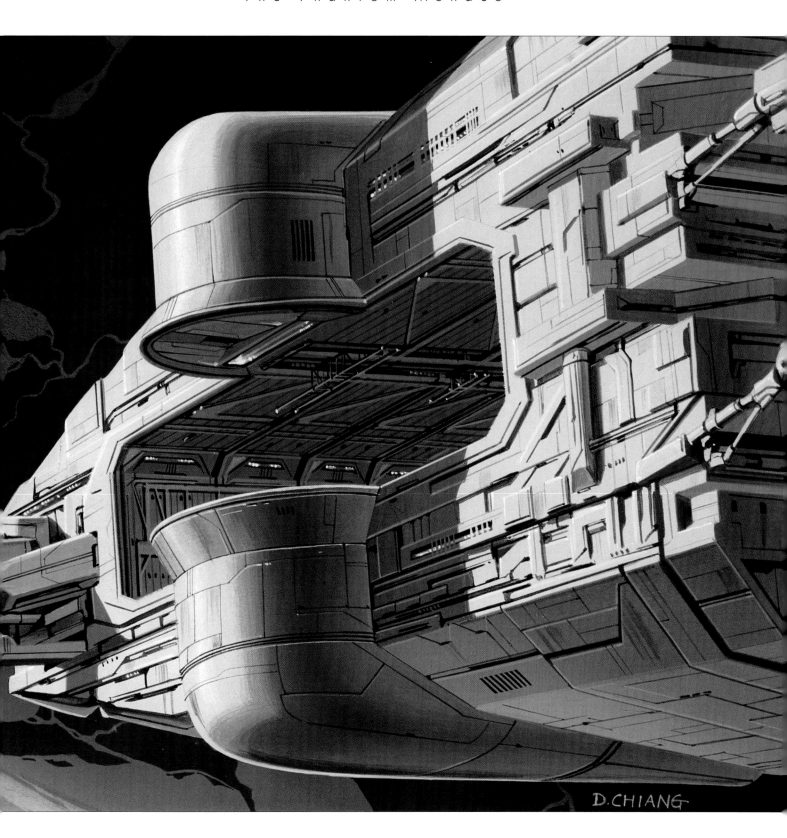

D.CHIANG

2

1

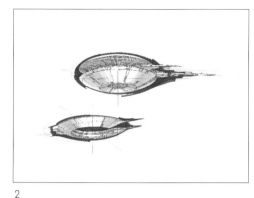

2

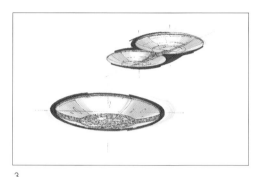

3

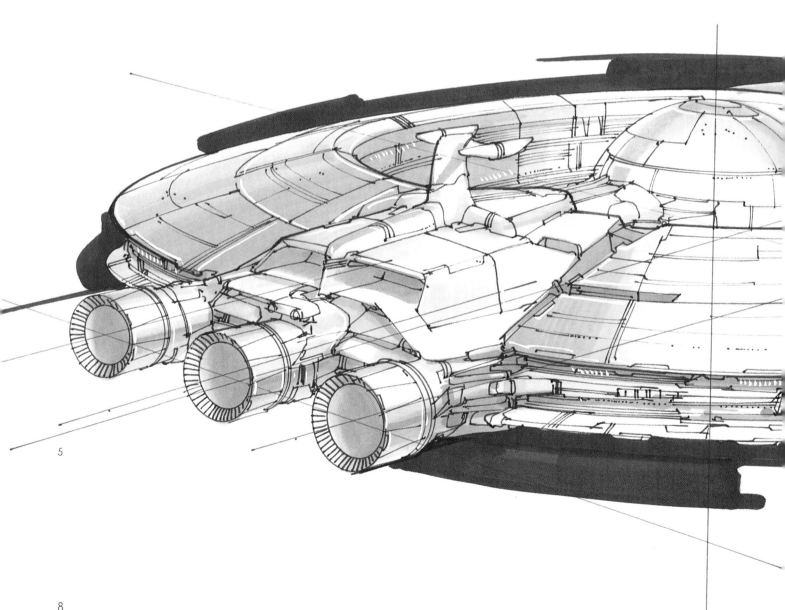

5

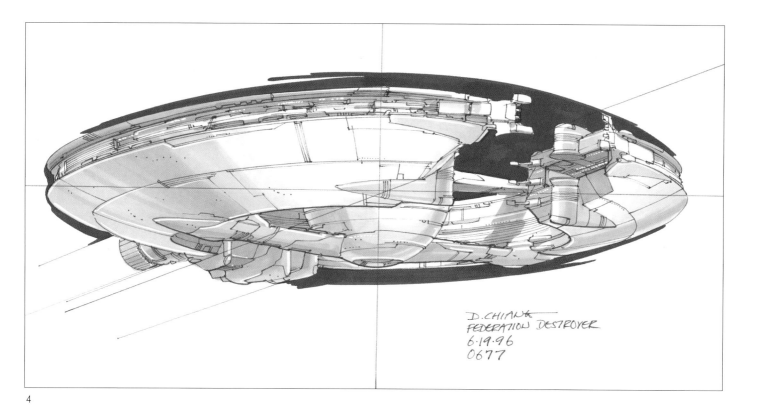

D.CHIANG
FEDERATION DESTROYER
6·19·96
0677

4

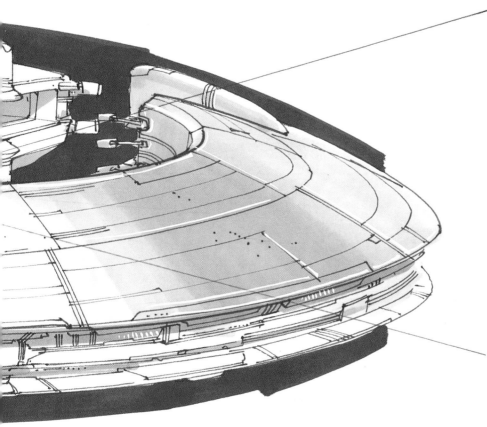

6

Trade Federation battleship, conceptual designs and model
1–5 Doug Chiang
6 John Goodson

Lucas wanted the battleship to have a retro-saucer look (1, 3) but felt it needed a distinct sense of front and rear. Chiang achieved this by adding the antennae and a docking section to one side, and a set of engines to the other (2). Lucas himself added the "bridge ball" to the center for the finished design (4–6).

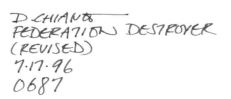

D.CHIANG
FEDERATION DESTROYER
(REVISED)
7·17·96
0687

1

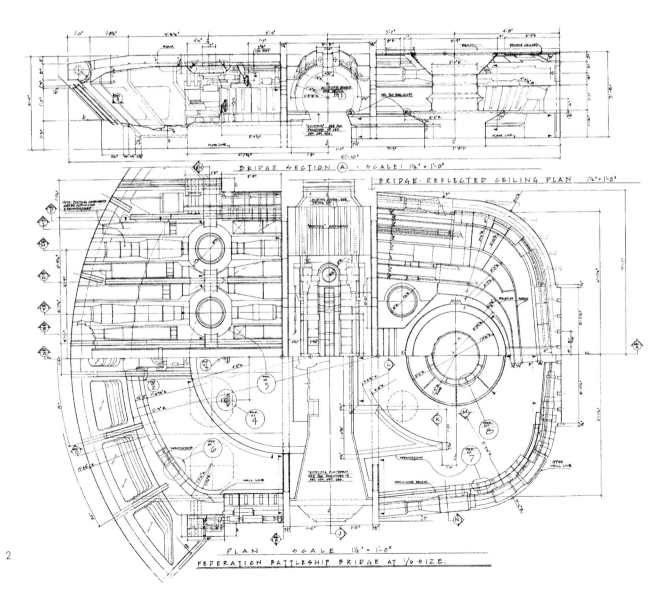

2

BRIDGE SECTION Ⓐ · SCALE! 1½" = 1'-0"

BRIDGE · REFLECTED CEILING PLAN   1½" = 1'-0"

PLAN   SCALE 1½" = 1'-0"
FEDERATION BATTLESHIP BRIDGE AT ⅙ SIZE.

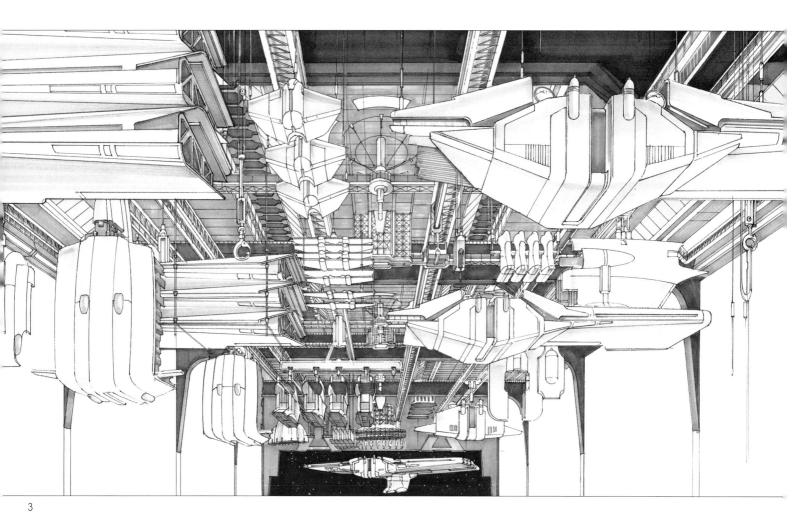

3

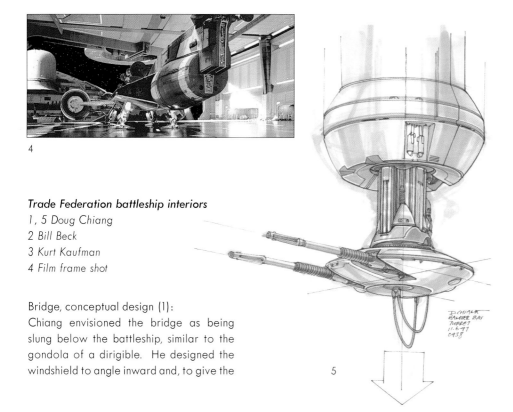

4

Trade Federation battleship interiors
1, 5 Doug Chiang
2 Bill Beck
3 Kurt Kaufman
4 Film frame shot

Bridge, conceptual design (1):
Chiang envisioned the bridge as being slung below the battleship, similar to the gondola of a dirigible. He designed the windshield to angle inward and, to give the

5

bridge the character of an old sailing ship, by adding the three steering wheels.

Bridge, technical drawing for production model construction (2):
Although parts of the bridge were built as sets and shot with human actors, others were built in miniature and shot as models at ILM. Architectural drawings were made for both versions. This one is for the miniature version.

Hangar, ceiling detail design for matte composite (3)

Hangar interior, finished shot (4)

Hangar turret gun, conceptual design (5):
This is the gun that drops down from the ceiling of the Trade Federation hangar and destroys the Republic Cruiser, *Radiant VII*.

1

2

3

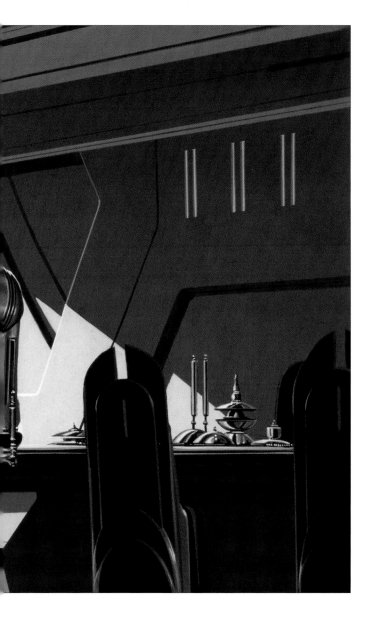

4

5

6

Trade Federation battleship interiors
1, 2 Doug Chiang
3 Gavin Bocquet/production design department
4–6 Edwin Natividad

Obi-Wan and TC-3 (later renamed TC-14) in the conference room, production painting (1):
When this painting was done, the character of Qui-Gon had not yet been added to the story. Thus, in this illustration, Obi-Wan waits to meet with the representatives of the Trade Federation—alone.

Bridge, storyboard (2):
The bridge was later modified, after live action footage had been shot. The area in black represents a scene shot on a partial set. The footage was sent to Chiang, and he designed the rest of the bridge. The windows have been shrunk a bit from the previous design, so that they appear more armored and protected.

Conference room, foam core conceptual model (3):
Architectural models such as this one were built by the production design department at Leavesden Studios to give Lucas a sense of how the conference room set might look from various camera angles and under different lighting conditions.

Nute Gunray, Obi-Wan and Qui-Gon, TC-3, storyboards (4–6)

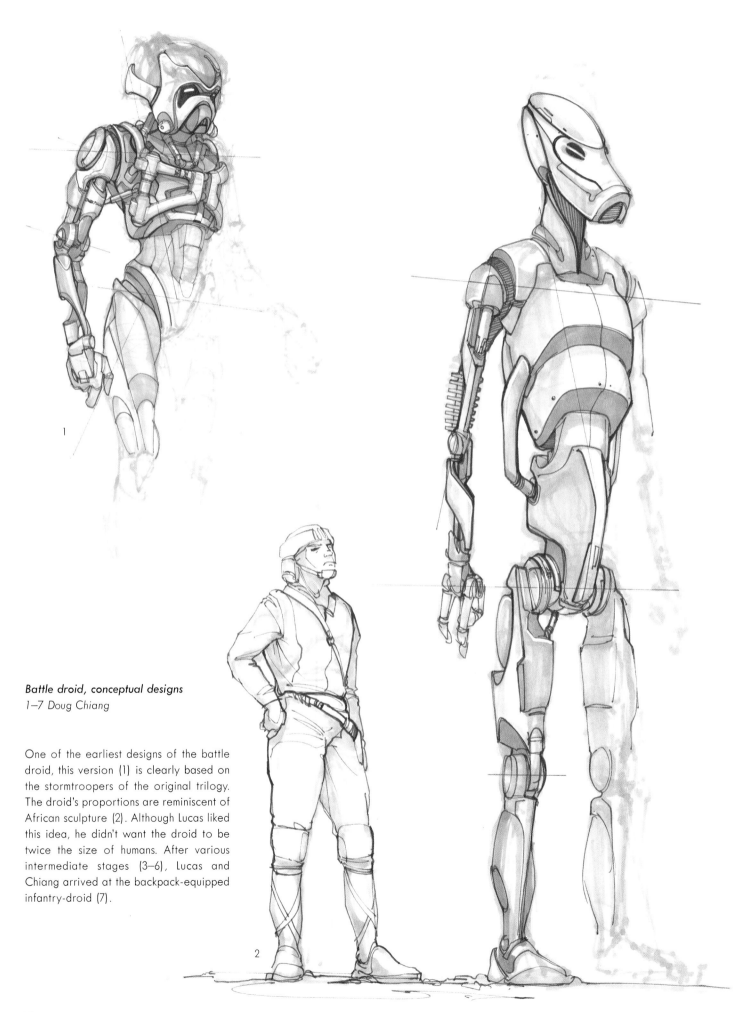

Battle droid, conceptual designs
1–7 Doug Chiang

One of the earliest designs of the battle droid, this version (1) is clearly based on the stormtroopers of the original trilogy. The droid's proportions are reminiscent of African sculpture (2). Although Lucas liked this idea, he didn't want the droid to be twice the size of humans. After various intermediate stages (3–6), Lucas and Chiang arrived at the backpack-equipped infantry-droid (7).

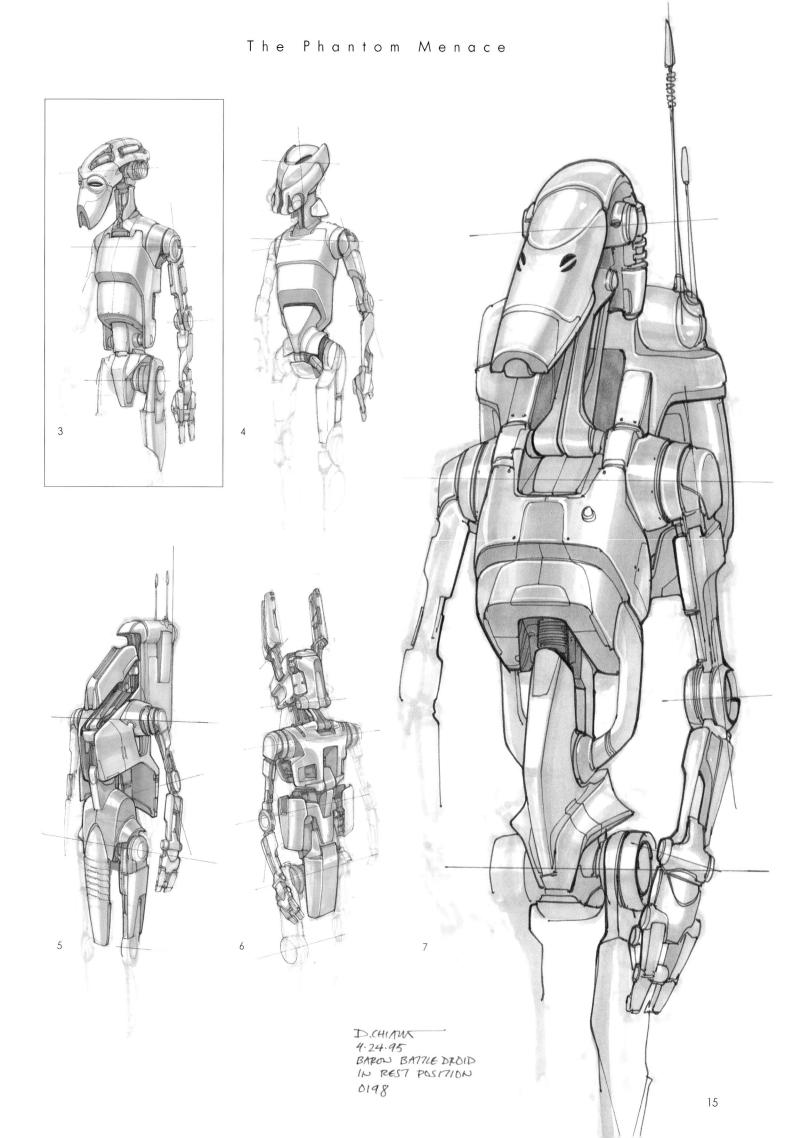

3

4

5

6

7

D. CHIANG
4·24·95
BARON BATTLE DROID
IN REST POSITION
0198

1

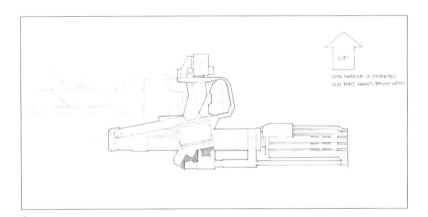

2

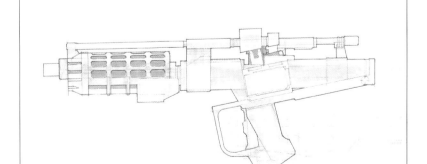

3

Battle droids and weaponry
1, 4–7 Doug Chiang
2, 3 Jay Shuster

The invasion of Naboo, conceptual designs (1, 7)

Blaster gun, initial and finished conceptual designs (2, 3)

Battle droid, alternate conceptual designs:
At one point, Chiang experimented with giving the droid another set of arms (4) to achieve a more multifunctional look. Another version gave the droids expanding body parts (5), while still another called for them to be able to fold up into rocket-packs and fly (6). While this last idea was not pursued, the folding configuration became the pattern for how the droids would be stored on the Multi Troop Transport (MTT) racks.

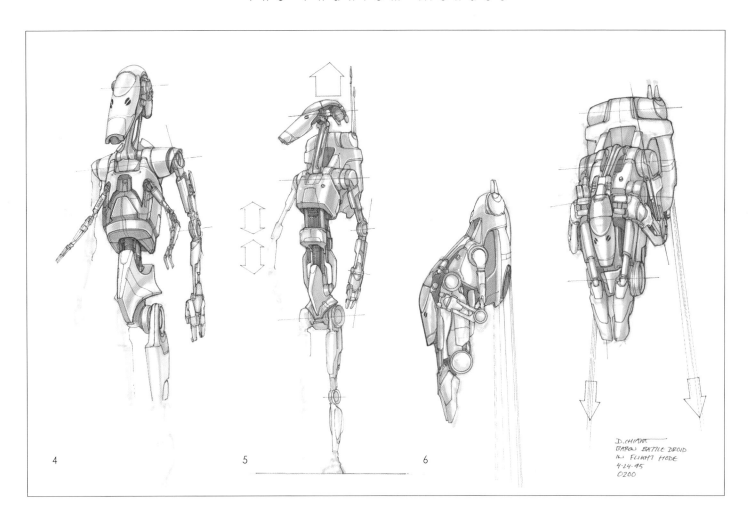

4   5   6

D. CHIANG
BARON BATTLE DROID
IN FLIGHT MODE
4-24-95
0200

7

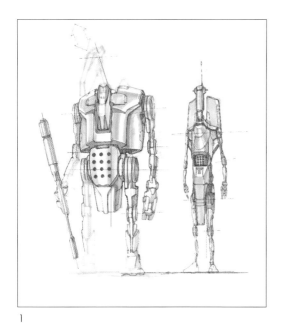

1

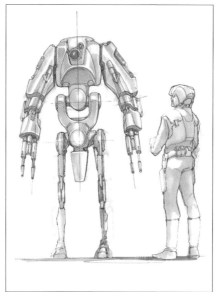

2

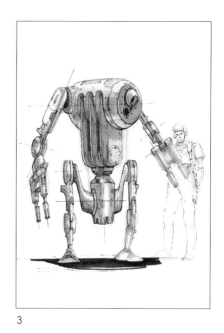

3

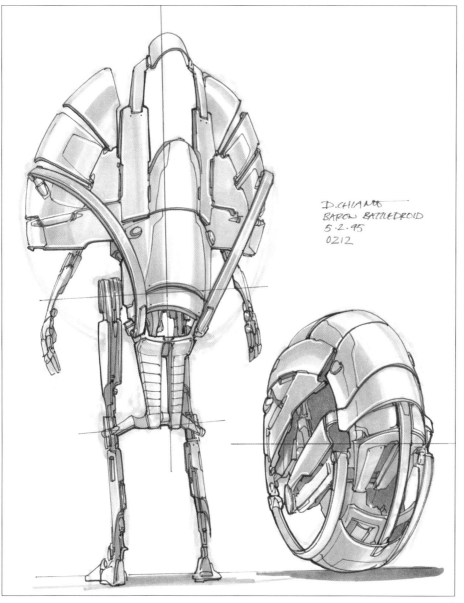

4

Droideka, conceptual designs
1–7 Doug Chiang

The droidekas started off as bulky battle droids (1–3). Soon, two divergent designs were being pursued: droids that could roll (4, 5, 7) and droids that couldn't (6).

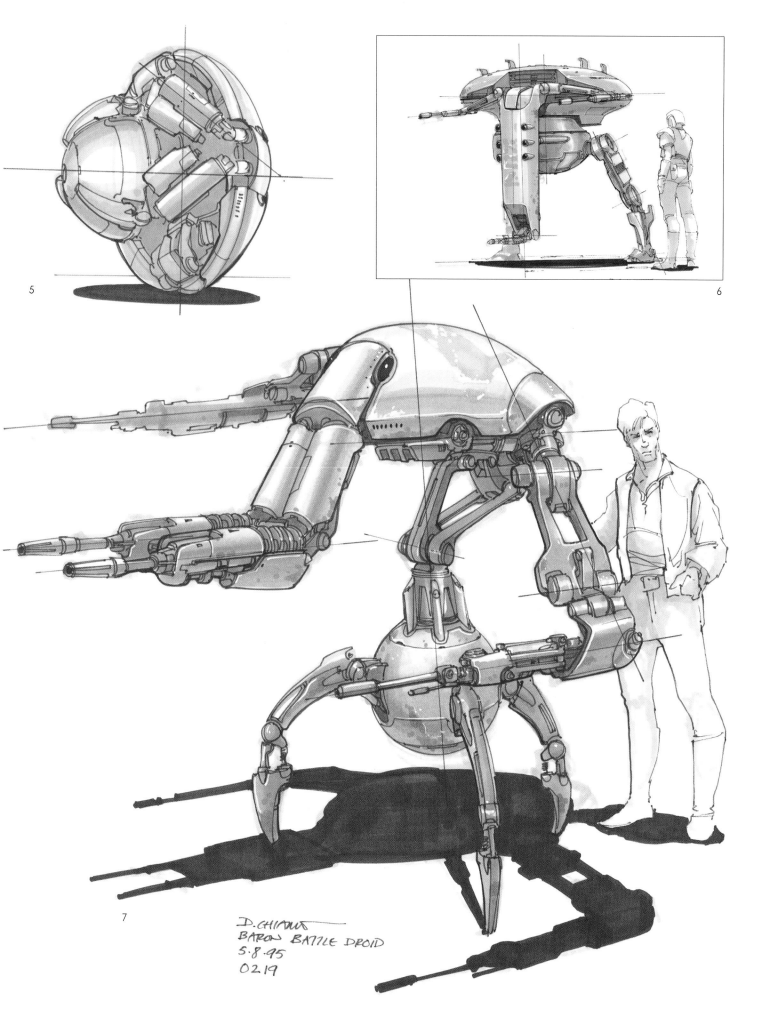

5

6

7

D. CHIANT
BARON BATTLE DROID
5.8.95
02.19

1

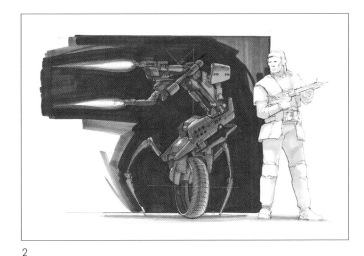

2

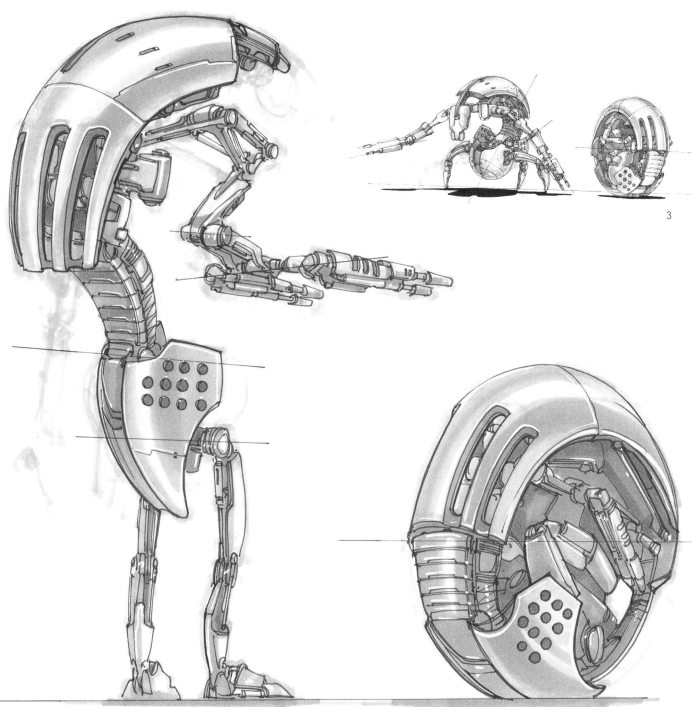

3

4

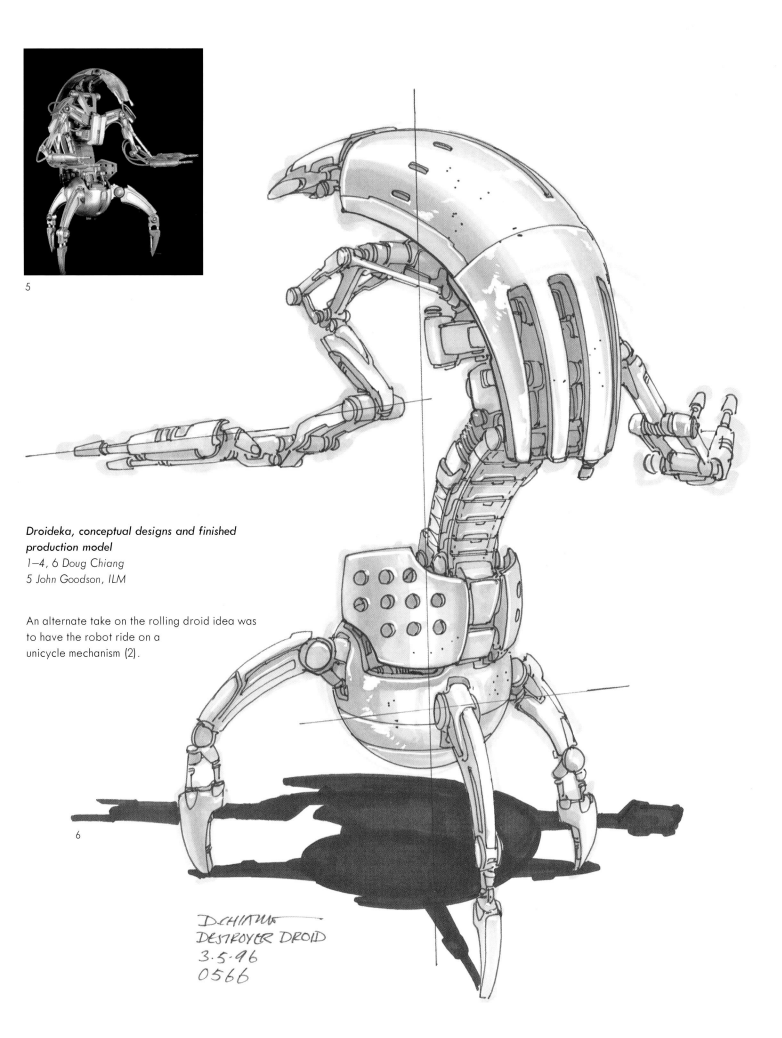

Droideka, conceptual designs and finished production model
1–4, 6 Doug Chiang
5 John Goodson, ILM

An alternate take on the rolling droid idea was to have the robot ride on a unicycle mechanism (2).

5

6

D.CHIANG
DESTROYER DROID
3.5.96
0566

1

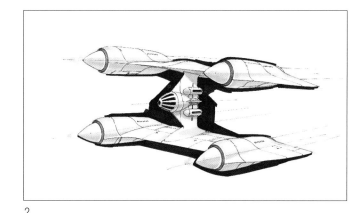

2

D. CHIANG
STARFIGHTER DROID
10·7·97
0923

3

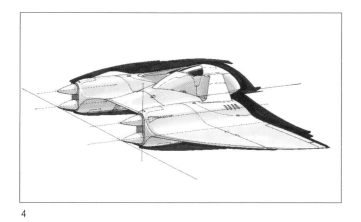

4

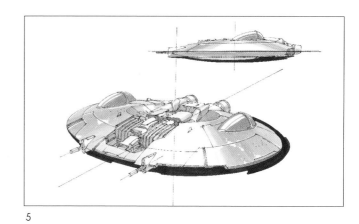

5

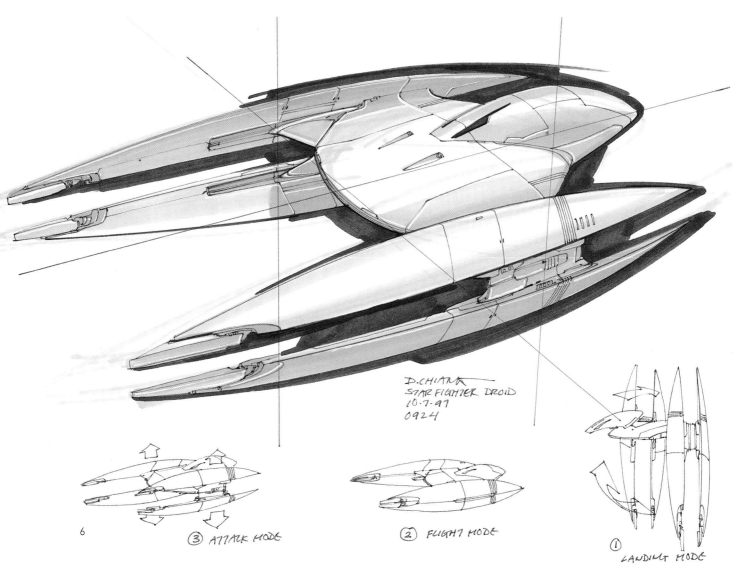

D.CHIANG
STAR FIGHTER DROID
10.7.97
0924

③ ATTACK MODE

② FLIGHT MODE

① LANDING MODE

6

Trade Federation starfighter droid,
conceptual design and model
1—6 Doug Chiang
7 John Goodson, ILM

Originally, these starfighters weren't droids, but had droid pilots. Early designs (1, 2, 4) were variations on the TIE fighter, leading to a version that was followed for much of the pre-production phase (5).

Lucas and Chiang then determined that the entire starfighter should itself be a droid. The finished version (3, 6), when in ship mode, becomes a reasonable precursor to the TIE fighter. In droid mode it exhibits the menacing look of a pterodactyl. The color scheme was finalized for this computer generated (CG) version of Goodson's conceptual model (7).

7

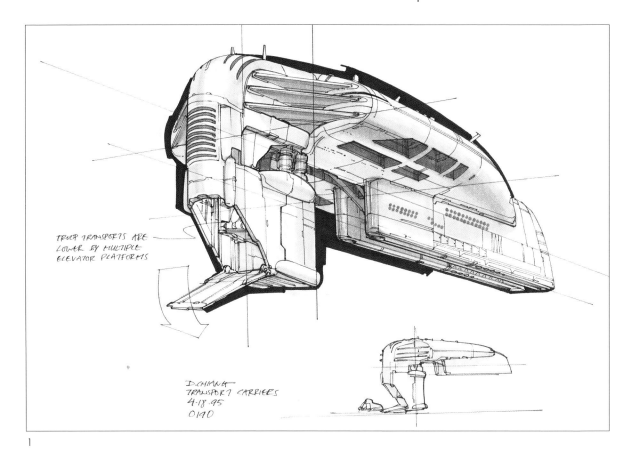

1

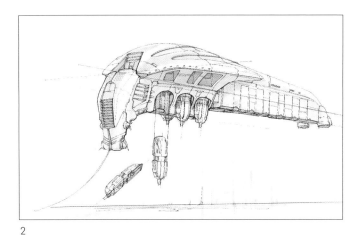

2

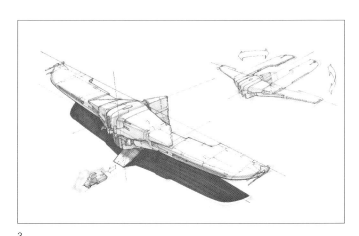

3

*Trade Federation landing ship, conceptual designs
and model*
1–3, 5, 6 Doug Chiang
4 John Goodson

Initially, the landing ship was more dirigible-like
(1). It hovered, a front hatch opened, and MTTs
were deployed. An alternate version lowered
the MTTs down in "cocoons" (2). However,
Lucas requested a more aggressive, imposing
appearance, so Chiang based his next design
on a ship's anchor, designing the vessel to trans-
form and unfold (3). As Chiang modified it further, he based the landing ship on a giant, pri-
mordial dragonfly (6). Lucas, however, assumed
that it was based on an old biplane and was

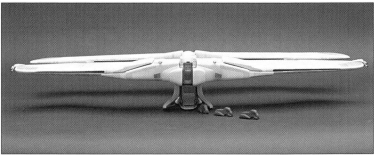

4

pleased with the retro-look. Either way, it
looked massive and menacing, and with a few
minor adjustments, the design was finished (4, 5).

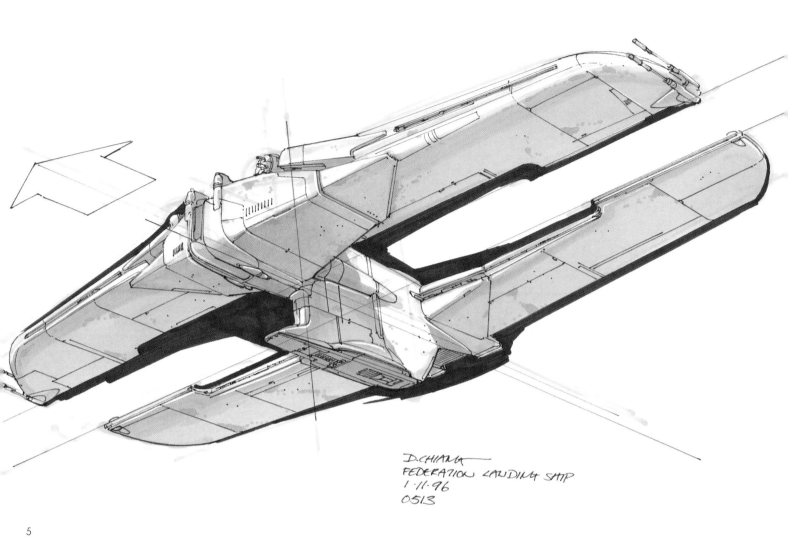

D.CHIANG
FEDERATION LANDING SHIP
1·11·96
0513

5

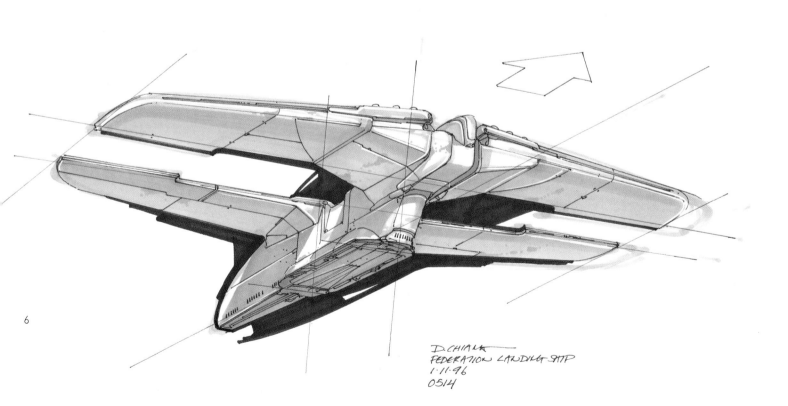

D.CHIANG
FEDERATION LANDING SHIP
1·11·96
0514

6

1

**Trade Federation landing ships, production
painting and animatic frame**
1 Doug Chiang
2 Evan Pontoriero

D. CHIANG

2

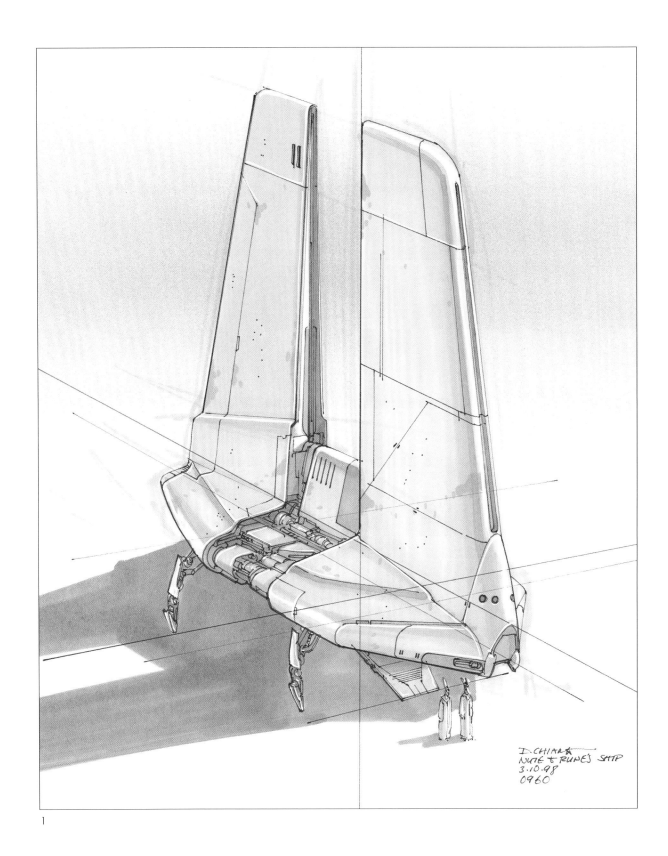

1

Nute and Rune's shuttle, conceptual designs
1–3 Doug Chiang

First, Chiang created a small, vertical-winged version of the landing ship (1). He then refined and curved the wings, and designed the landing gear to be permanently extended, thus enhancing the ship's insectlike appearance (2). Lucas liked this design, but asked that one of the wings be eliminated, resulting in the finished sketch (3).

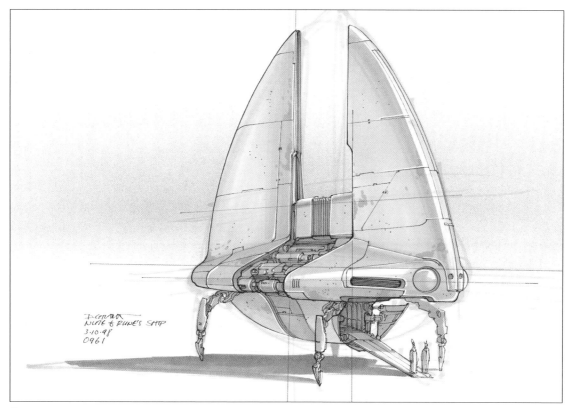

2

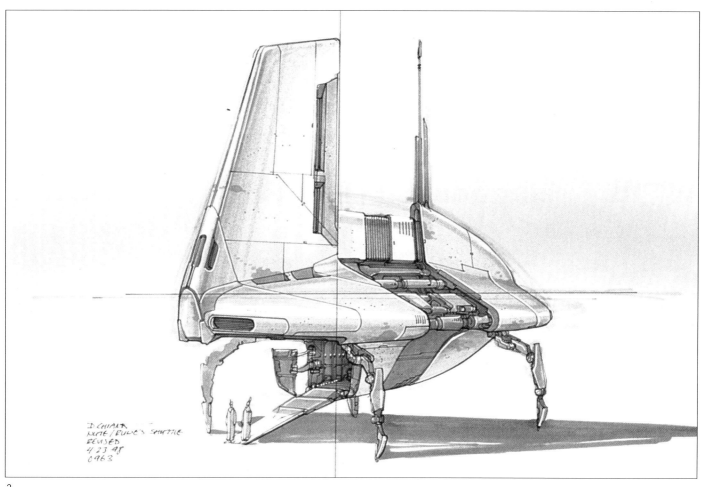

3

1

Multi Troop Transport (MTT)
1, 2, 4–7 Doug Chiang
3 John Duncan, ILM

Battle droids scouting the MTT landing area, conceptual design (1)

Deployment of droid dispersal rack, conceptual design (2)

MTT, finished production model (3)

MTT, conceptual designs:
Lucas wanted a huge, hovering, locomotive-type vehicle that would charge through the swamp, knocking down everything in its path, so Chiang created an initial battering ram–like design. After experimenting with a more literal locomotive look, which he stylized to resemble the barrel of a revolver (5), Chiang began to draw on another animal influence—the elephant—giving the MTT a high "forehead" and gun turret "tusks" (4). Lucas was quite fond of this design, and Chiang refined it a bit more to create the final version (7).

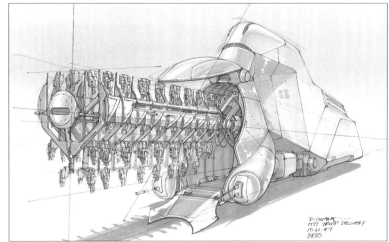

2

3

4

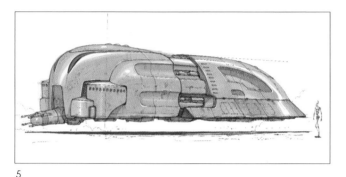

5

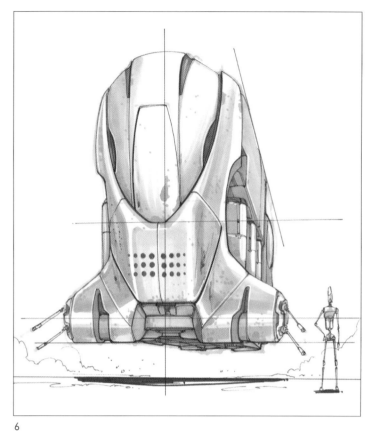

6

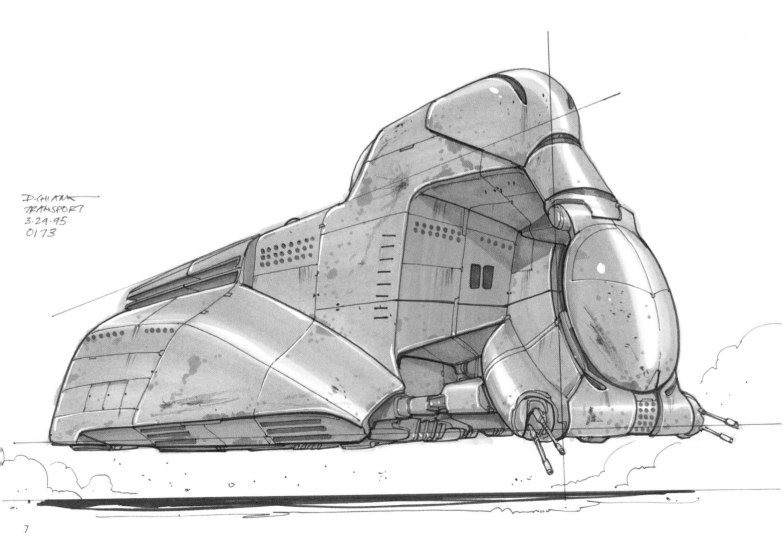

D. CHIAN
TRANSPORT
3.29.95
0173

7

1

MTTs invading Naboo, production paintings

1, 2 Doug Chiang

In this version of the swamp chase (2), Jar Jar and Obi-Wan are chased by the MTT—not Jar Jar and Qui-Gon. Qui-Gon had yet to be added to the cast.

2

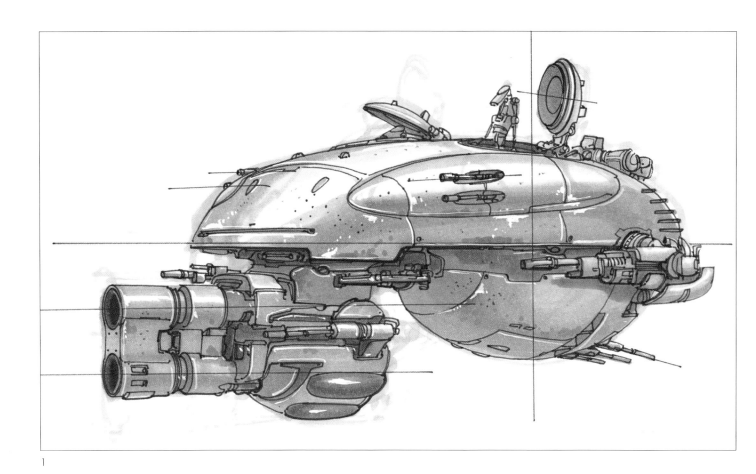

1

2

3

Armored Attack Tank (AAT), conceptual designs
1–5 Doug Chiang

Lucas wanted the AAT to be the Trade Federation's attack helicopter—essentially a big, fast, low-flying gun. These first two versions (1, 2) were too armor-heavy and ponderous. Lucas liked the animalistic elements of a subsequent design, particularly the large "arms" on either side (3), but he was also fond of the "big flying iron" (4). The large front platform was ideal for shearing down trees, and the greater width enhanced its banking and rolling as it flew. Chiang ultimately combined the two to create the finished version, throwing in a few lionlike traits, such as the gun turret "claws" (5).

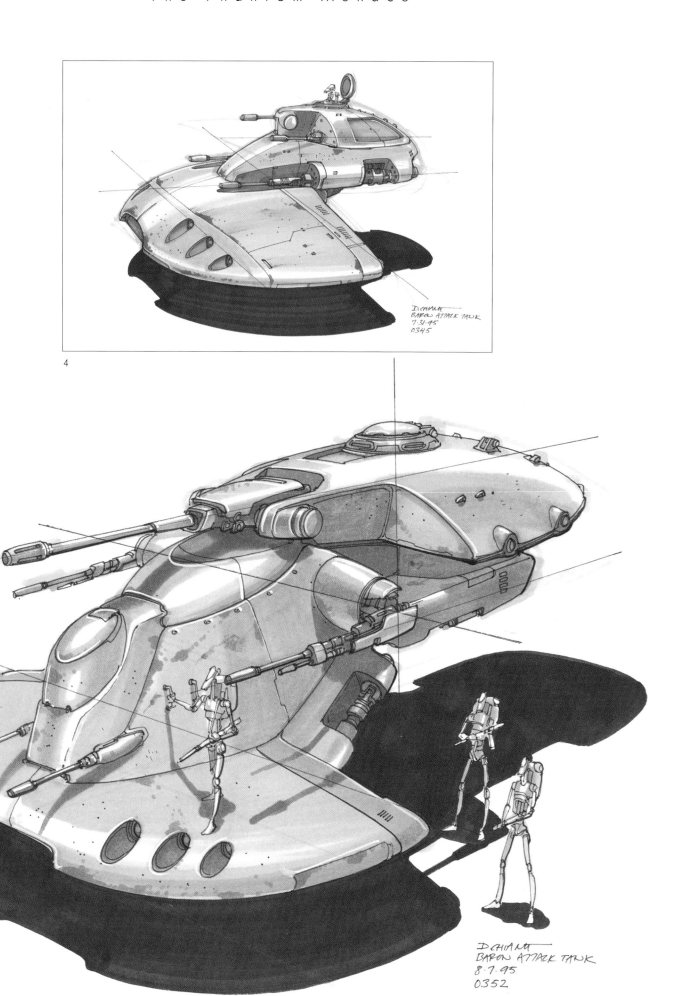

4

DCHIANG
BARON ATTACK TANK
7·31·95
0345

5

DCHIANG
BARON ATTACK TANK
8·7·95
0352

1

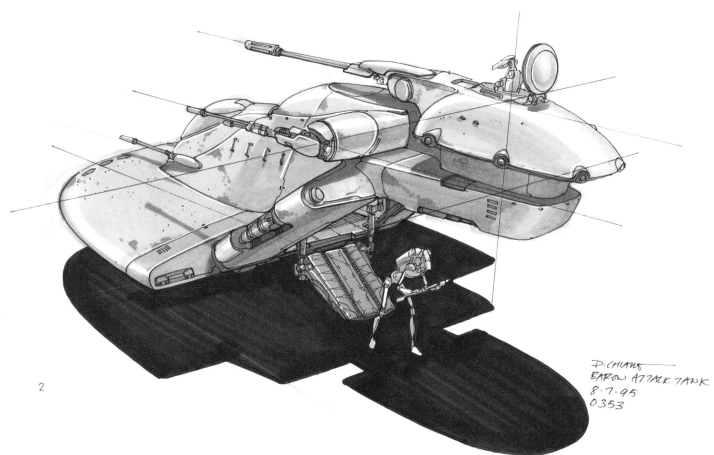

2

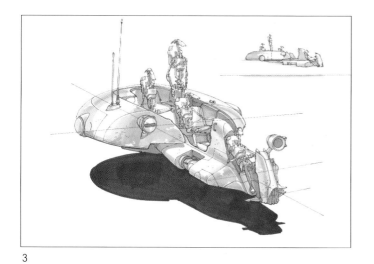

3

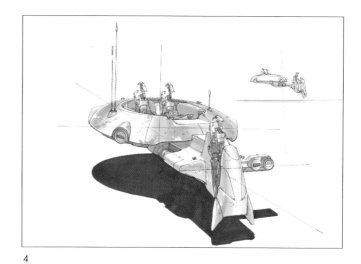

4

Battle droid ground vehicles
1–4 Doug Chiang
5 Jay Shuster

Battle droids atop an AAT, conceptual design (1)

AAT, finished conceptual design, back view (2)

These speeder designs (3, 4) were to be used by commander droids to cruise up and down the battle lines. They were never used in the film. When Lucas requested a droid rack that would be carried on a repulsorlift sled, Shuster turned the speeder into a troop carrier by scaling out the back to accommodate the droid rack (5).

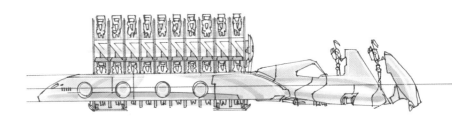

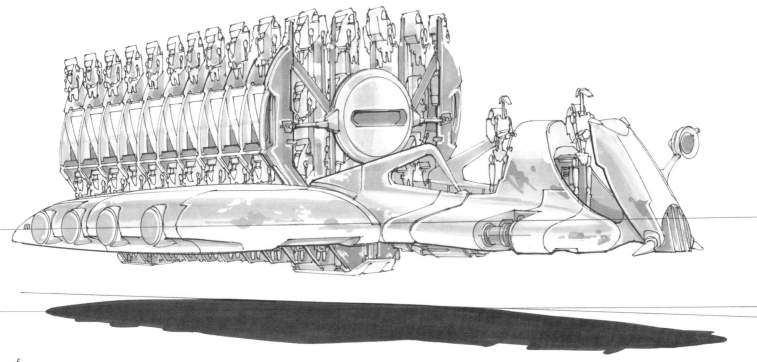

5

1

Droid/Gungan battle
1, 2 Doug Chiang

Trade Federation vanguard, production painting (1)

In an early draft of the script, the Gungans were to have a fleet of flying mounts called "air whales," which are an homage to Ralph McQuarrie's "thrantas" from his work on Cloud City. Their Trade Federation counterparts were to be droid-piloted "air bikes" (2) that were based on aphids. Although these air bikes were eliminated, along with the air whales, their influence is still seen in Darth Maul's speeder.

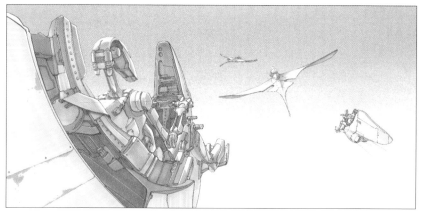

2

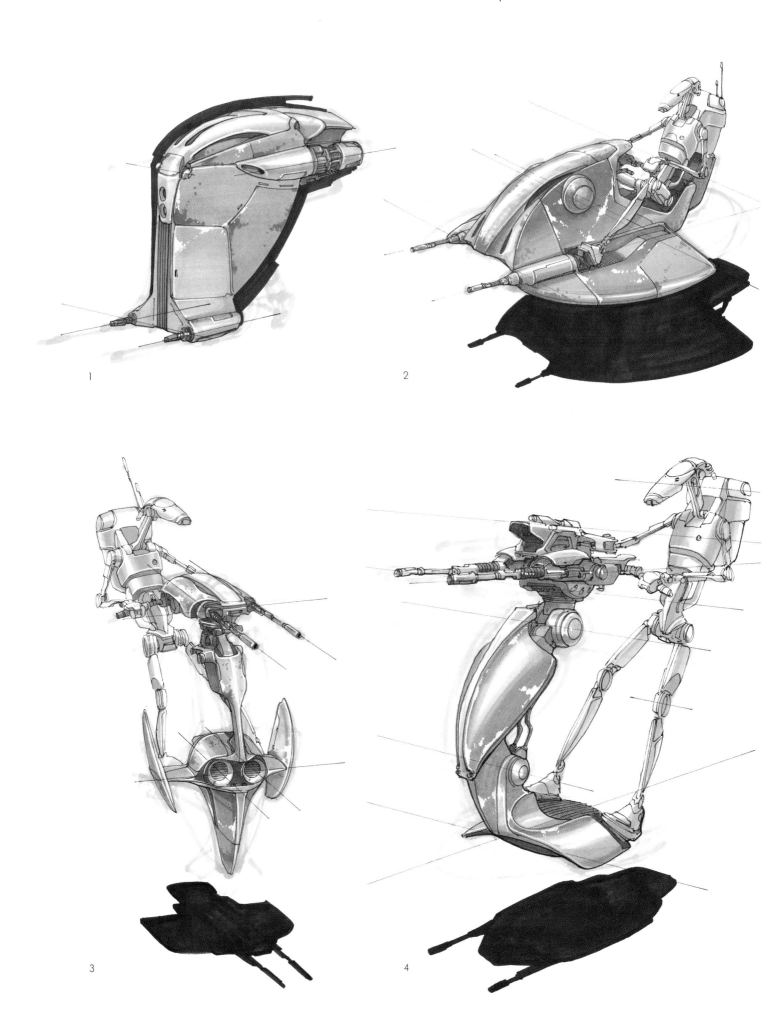

1

2

3

4

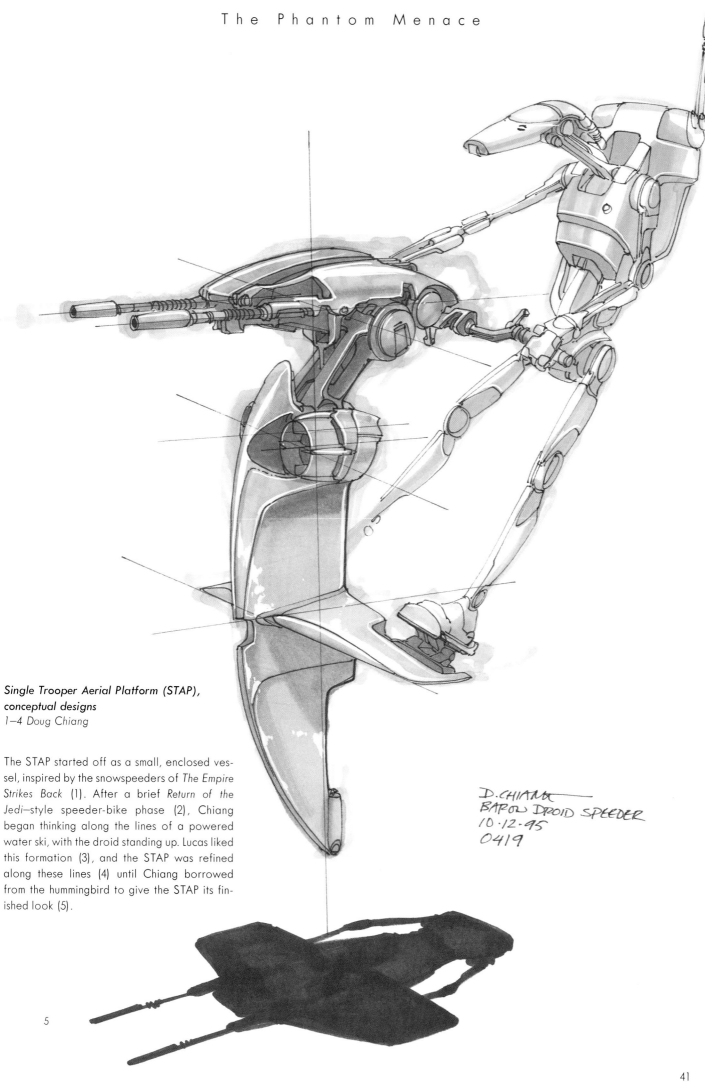

**Single Trooper Aerial Platform (STAP),
conceptual designs**
1–4 Doug Chiang

The STAP started off as a small, enclosed vessel, inspired by the snowspeeders of *The Empire Strikes Back* (1). After a brief *Return of the Jedi*–style speeder-bike phase (2), Chiang began thinking along the lines of a powered water ski, with the droid standing up. Lucas liked this formation (3), and the STAP was refined along these lines (4) until Chiang borrowed from the hummingbird to give the STAP its finished look (5).

D. CHIANG
BARON DROID SPEEDER
10·12·95
0419

5

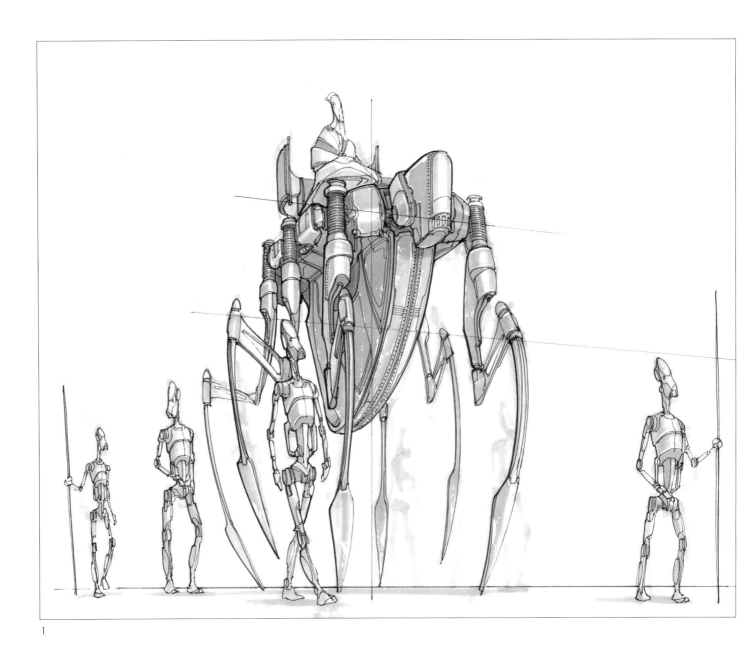

1

Nute Gunray
1–5 Doug Chiang

Walking throne, conceptual designs:
At one point, a hovering throne (2) was considered instead of the walking thrones (1, 4, 5). The overall intent of this sketch (2) was to give Nute the appearance of an emperor, with a full military escort.

Neimoidian head, conceptual design:
The Neimodians were designed after the look of the battle droids had been finalized. On the assumption that the Neimoidians had created the droids in their own image, the Neimoidians were given correspondingly elongated heads (3). That look was maintained up until shooting, when, due to various considerations, a more human-shaped head was adopted.

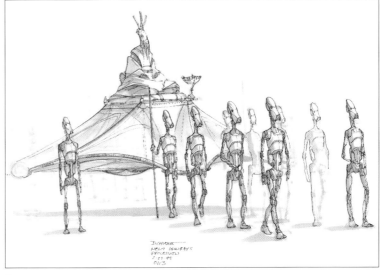

2

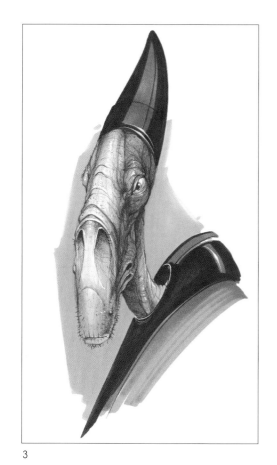

3

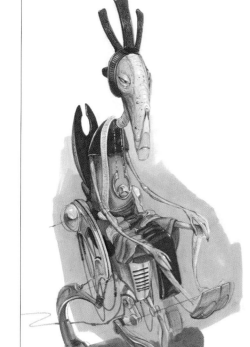

4

5

D CHIANG
BARON LORD IN
"WALKING THRONE"
2·24·95
O111

D. CHIANG

1

Nute Gunray's troop inspection
1, 2 Doug Chiang

Surveying the captured Theed hangar, production painting (1)

The Trade Federation landing ship hangar on the eve of invasion, conceptual design (2):
When this sketch was drawn, Lucas had yet to describe the scene, so Chiang began toying with

some ideas of his own, and ultimately, this sketch evolved into a key production painting (1). According to Chiang, "This image demonstrates the design philosophy of Episode I: combine different textures and styles to create a timeless whole. The hangar's old stone architecture is contrasted against the chrome starfighters and the unusual technology of the Trade Federation. All these elements come together to create a fantastic, yet convincing, fictional reality."

2

IAIN M·CAIG
NIMOIDIAN DESIGNS
10 . 10 . 96 .   RUNE.

DOFINE

1

2

3

46

4

Neimoidian physique and costume, conceptual designs
1–5 Iain McCaig

For the Neimoidian costumes, McCaig researched ancient Egypt and the Japanese kabuki to create rich, flowing robes that the Neimoidians would wear in an attempt to offset their shriveled bodies. For their headpieces, he studied African masks and totems. To evoke a particularly decadent look, McCaig gave them white makeup and moles.

5

The Planet of
Naboo

The lush, fertile planet of Naboo is dominated by two species: the humanoid Naboo and the amphibious Gungans. Though there is a symbiotic relationship that exists between the two species, the Gungans and the Naboo regard each other with suspicion and mistrust.

The human-dominated region has a sunny, Mediterranean look to it, and is characterized by rushing, whitewater rivers, rolling green hills, and endless, grassy plains. The population is fairly sparse and resides largely in an ecologically conscious city-state called Theed; a paradise of a city, free of industrial pollutants.

Just as beautiful is the Gungan region, which is dominated by beautiful bayous and is teeming with animal life. The Gungans live in an underwater community called Otoh Gunga that resembles a vast, brilliantly hued coral reef, although they occasionally venture upward to a part of a swamp they consider to be sacred. This sacred swamp is dotted with enormous humanoid sculptures, left behind by a long-dead species that predates the Gungans and the Naboo.

The Trade Federation covets the planet Naboo for its vast resources and for its strategic location along the Galactic Trade Routes. Thinking the planet to be defenseless, the Neimoidians fiendishly deploy the cold, metallic might of their mechanized militia in an attempt to turn the biotic, bucolic world into a droid-dominated dictatorship. With the Republic mired in bureaucracy and unable to help, the Naboo and the Gungans must learn to work together in order to rid themselves of the Neimoidian occupation. They succeed spectacularly—much to the surprise and dismay of the Trade Federation, the outnumbered amphibians and anthropoids triumph over the armaments and androids.

Naboo

Otoh Gunga

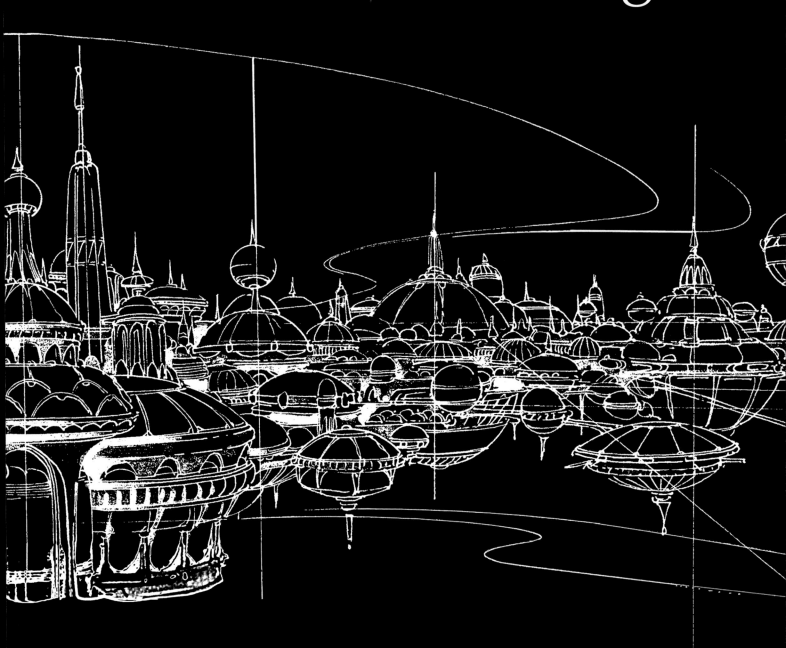

A tour of the Lucasfilm offices at Skywalker Ranch immediately reveals that George Lucas is a devotee of the art nouveau style. All the light fixtures and wall sconces are crafted in a graceful, flowery, and curvilinear fashion. Lucas wanted Otoh Gunga to display a similar look, describing the city as a luminescent, crystalline chandelier made up of glass bubbles, submerged deep beneath the seas of Naboo.

Art nouveau originated at the end of the nineteenth century in response to that era's rampant industrialization. Given the nature of the Naboo/Neimoidian conflict, it made sense to base the Gungan's aboriginal culture on such a style. Gungan technology is animal-based; they utilize very little in the way of machinery. As a result, their works are hand-tooled and heavily influenced by their aquatic surroundings, and this stands out in stark contrast to the mass-produced mechanization of the Trade Federation.

The art department had to figure out how such a supposedly primitive culture could create a dazzling, majestic bubble city without resorting to the use of advanced machinery. Clearly the Gungans had to walk a fine line. They couldn't be too advanced, yet they had to be skilled enough to harvest energy and materials from their surroundings. Lucas himself suggested a loophole: just because the Gungans didn't know how to synthesize technology, this didn't necessarily mean they wouldn't know how to grow it organically.

Thus, Otoh Gunga "grew" out of the idea that the Gungans could manipulate their environment to create force field bubbles, and anchor them to the side of an underwater cliff. The city would draw on some mysterious, photo-phosphorescent, bioelectric energy. Thus they could become a power to contend with, without altering or compromising their animal-based culture.

Since the Gungans were meant to live in harmony with nature as opposed to imposing their will upon it, Lucas insisted that the city's bubble support struts, or "ribs," be downplayed. The bubbles themselves were to be the strongest element, a kaleidoscopic mix of colors that make the city look almost magical. Each generation of Gungans would add bubbles to those of their ancestors. As a result, viewed from the top, the city would look like a continually branching tree or—more appropriately—a coral reef. In fact, plenty of coral growth would accumulate on the bubble support ribs, and mini reefs would have cropped up around the city, adding an overall coral-like texture.

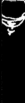

Gungan weaponry was designed to be consistent with the city's architecture, and was also inspired by coral, crustacean, and seashell formations. Gungan energy weapons and shield generators were to draw on the same electro-organic technology as the bubble generators, and, like the rib supports, look as if they are hand-made.

Since the Gungans spend most of their time underwater or in swamps, they would have little need for automotive land craft. When moving around on land, the Gungans would use animal mounts. As for underwater transport, the submarine used by Gungan Jar Jar Binks and the Jedi represented yet another example of animal-influenced, bioelectrically-powered technology. Its design combines the body of a manta ray with the tentacles of a squid.

Gungan clothing had to allow for movement on land and water. Since the Gungans themselves would be completely computer-generated, its development had to take into consideration ease of digital creation. Close-fitting leather proved to be the best bet, and it made sense from a cultural standpoint, given the Gungans' reliance on nature. From a technical standpoint, it saved the animators from having to simulate wrinkles and creases. And to fit in with the magical look of the culture, Doug Chiang gave the clothing a hint of an iridescent, seashell feel.

As the story unfolded, this "primitive" culture was vastly underestimated by the Trade Federation, and a favorite theme of the Star Wars films was continued. The natural, organic strength of the Gungans would prevail over the mechanized might of the Neimoidians.

1

Otoh Gunga
1, 3–6 Doug Chiang
2 Gavin Bocquet/David Dozoretz

Early conceptual designs (1, 3–6) and digital model (2)

Pages 48–49: Planet Naboo, matte painting
Brian Flora

Pages 50–51: Otoh Gunga, conceptual drawing
Doug Chiang

2

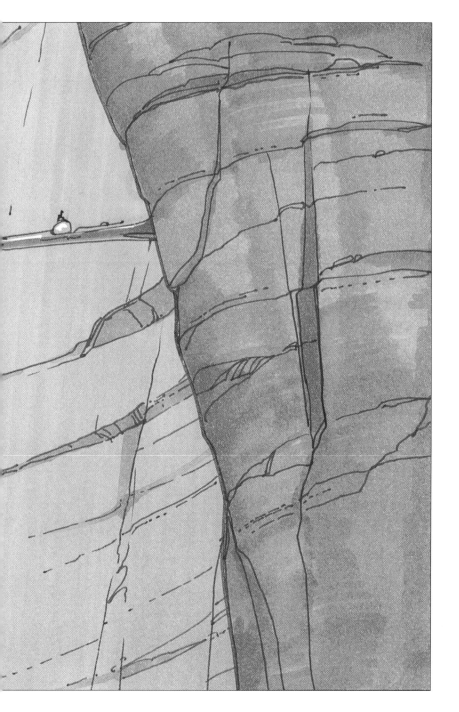

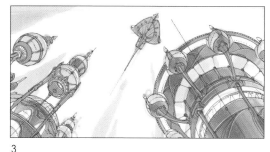

3

4

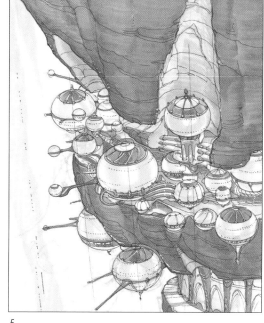

5

6

1

Otoh Gunga
1 Doug Chiang
2—4 Gavin Bocquet/production design department

Bongo submarine leaving the city, production
painting (1):
The first vision of Otoh Gunga gave the impres-
sion of an underwater chandelier, complete
with a school of kaadus swimming by.

Otoh Gunga council chambers, foam core conceptual models (2—4)

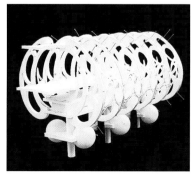

2

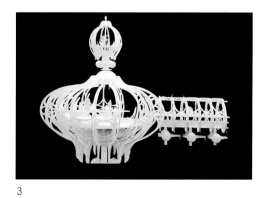

3

4

1

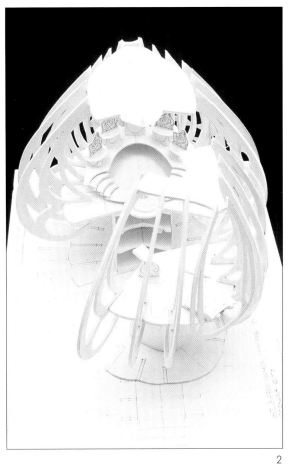

2

3

5

6

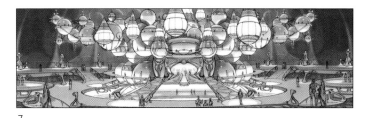

7

8

4

***Otoh Gunga* plaza**

1, 4, 5, 8 Marc Gabbana
3 Brian Flora
*2, 6 Gavin Bocquet/production design depart-
ment*
7 Marc Gabbana/Doug Chiang

Plaza, conceptual designs:
Originally, the plaza started off as a city square, with no strong outside perimeter. Lucas liked the mysterious mood seen in an early sketch (1), particularly the inky darkness outside and the little pools of light inside. Another preliminary design (5) was notable for its meandering walkways and coral formations. The city floor was open to the sea, allowing a nice glow to come from underneath, in addition to the coral that grew up, around, and through the city, but this element was eliminated in later designs (7, 8).

Council chambers, foam core conceptual models (2, 6)

Plaza, finished matte with storyboard painting (3, 4)

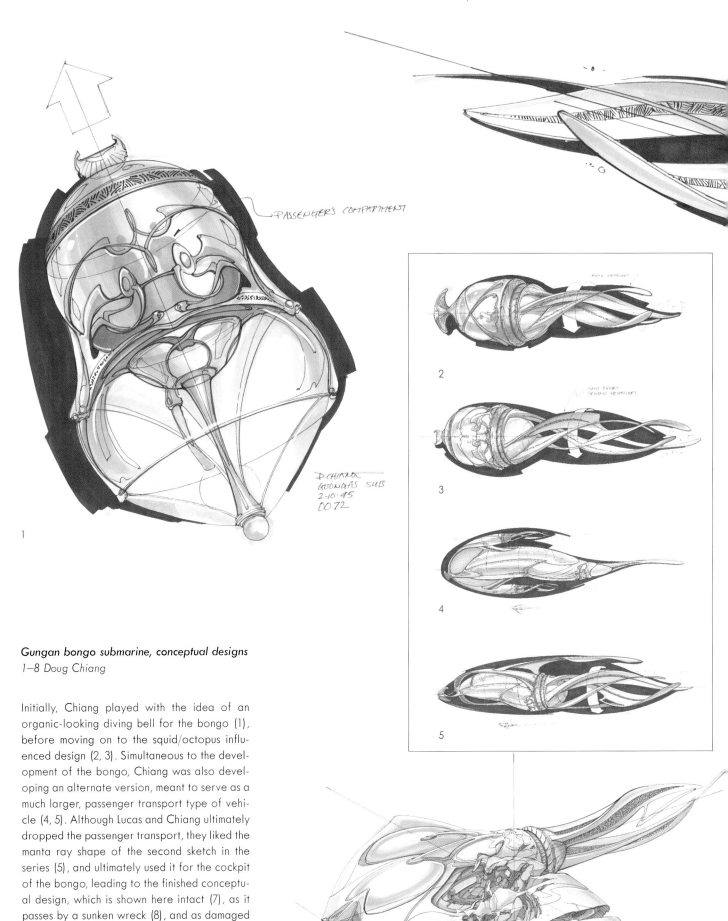

PASSENGER'S COMPARTMENT

Gungan bongo submarine, conceptual designs
1–8 Doug Chiang

Initially, Chiang played with the idea of an organic-looking diving bell for the bongo (1), before moving on to the squid/octopus influenced design (2, 3). Simultaneous to the development of the bongo, Chiang was also developing an alternate version, meant to serve as a much larger, passenger transport type of vehicle (4, 5). Although Lucas and Chiang ultimately dropped the passenger transport, they liked the manta ray shape of the second sketch in the series (5), and ultimately used it for the cockpit of the bongo, leading to the finished conceptual design, which is shown here intact (7), as it passes by a sunken wreck (8), and as damaged by the opee sea killer (6).

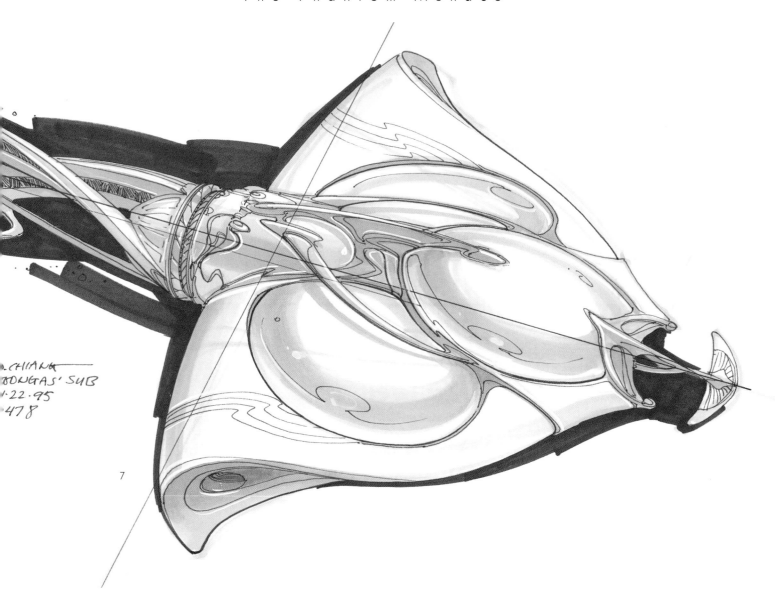

CHIANG
JONGAS' SUB
1·22·95
478

7

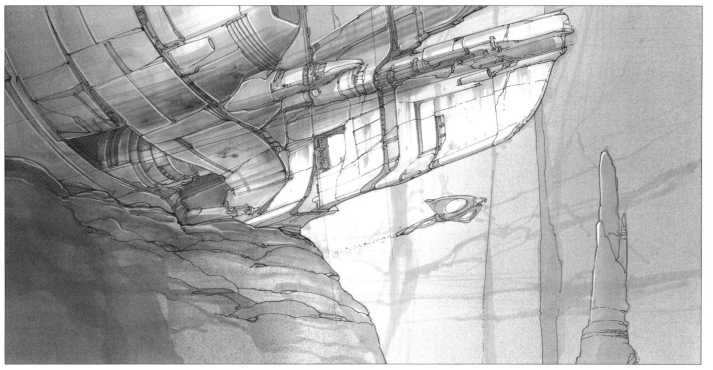

8

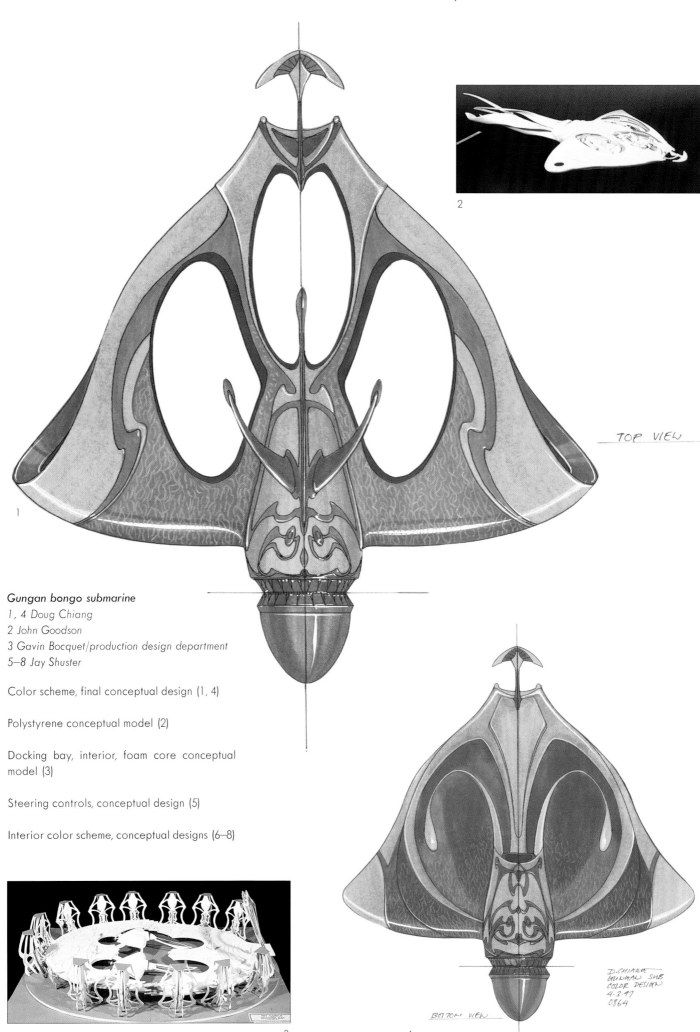

TOP VIEW

Gungan bongo submarine

1, 4 Doug Chiang

2 John Goodson

3 Gavin Bocquet/production design department

5—8 Jay Shuster

Color scheme, final conceptual design (1, 4)

Polystyrene conceptual model (2)

Docking bay, interior, foam core conceptual model (3)

Steering controls, conceptual design (5)

Interior color scheme, conceptual designs (6—8)

D. CHIANG
GUNGAN SUB
COLOR DESIGN
4.3.97
0864

BOTTOM VIEW

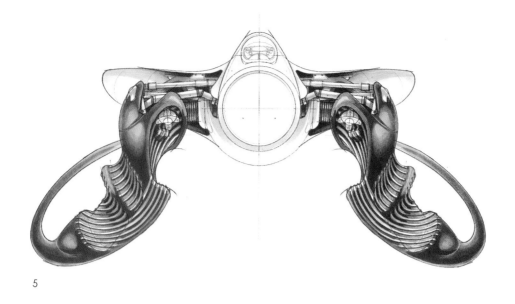

5

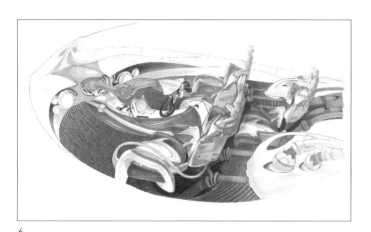

6

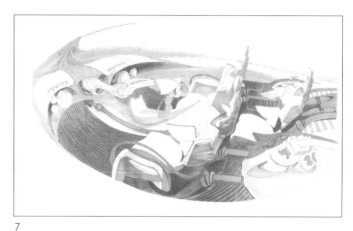

7

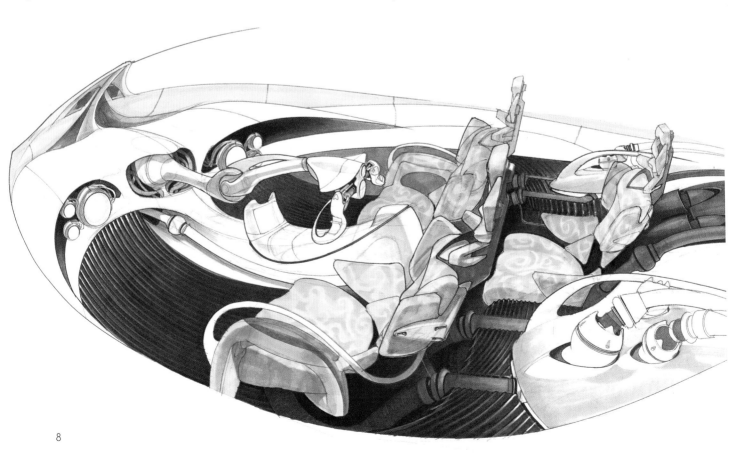

8

1

2

Opee sea killer
1–3, 5 Doug Chiang
4 Tony McVey
6 Terryl Whitlatch

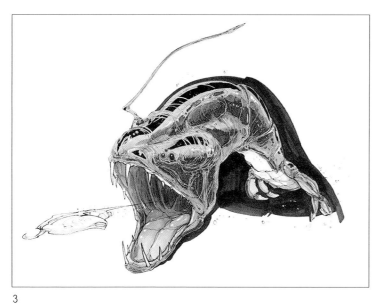

3

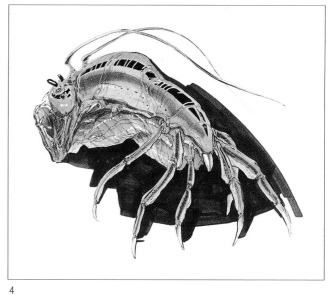

4

Conceptual designs:
At first, the opee sea killer was essentially a huge jaw grafted onto a fish/crab body (1). A second version (2) combined the traits of a crab with some mammalian characteristics, but ultimately, the opee became more of a cross between an anglerfish and a crab (3).

Sculpey concept maquette (4)

Opee sea killer pursuing the bongo, production painting (5)

Miscellaneous sea life, early conceptual designs (6)

5

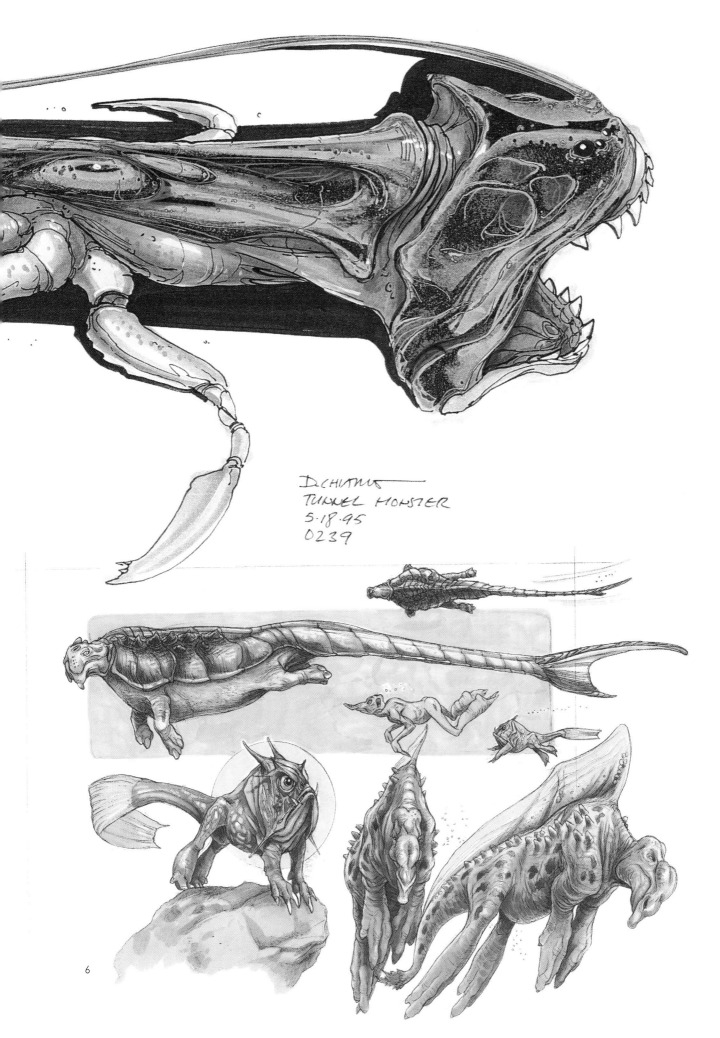

DICHYATUS
TUNNEL MONSTER
5·18·95
0239

6

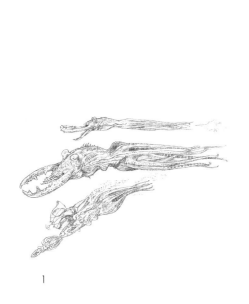

1

Colo claw fish, sando aqua monster, and opee sea killer
1–4, 6, 7 Terryl Whitlatch
5 Tony McVey

Colo claw fish, conceptual designs:
Whitlatch wanted the colo to have an invertebrate look, so she based it on a squid, an octopus, and an earwig (1). Later, she redesigned it with a bit of crocodile and moray eel thrown in (2–4).

Colo claw fish, cast resin concept maquette (5):
While many concept sculptures are made from Super Sculpey, it becomes brittle upon hardening. Thus, for greater permanence, sculptors will make a silicon mold from the Sculpey model, and then make a much more durable cast out of resin.

Sando aqua monster (6):
Whitlatch originally gave the sando a blue coloration scheme, reasoning that in the *Star Wars* universe, blue is often associated with the good guys (the good guys wield blue lightsabers, R2-D2 is blue, et cetera). She therefore thought that the Sando should be blue, since it saves Jar Jar and the Jedi from the opee sea killer.

Sando aqua monster and opee sea killer, motion studies (7)

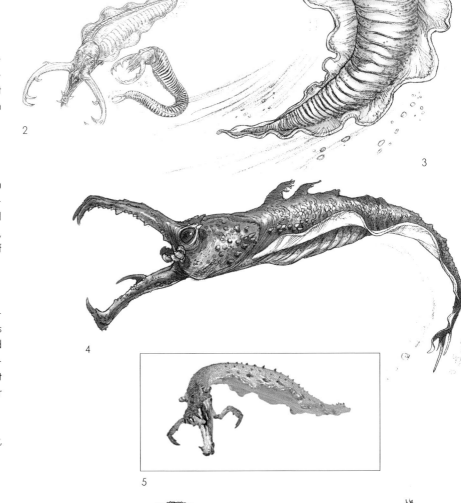

2

3

4

5

6

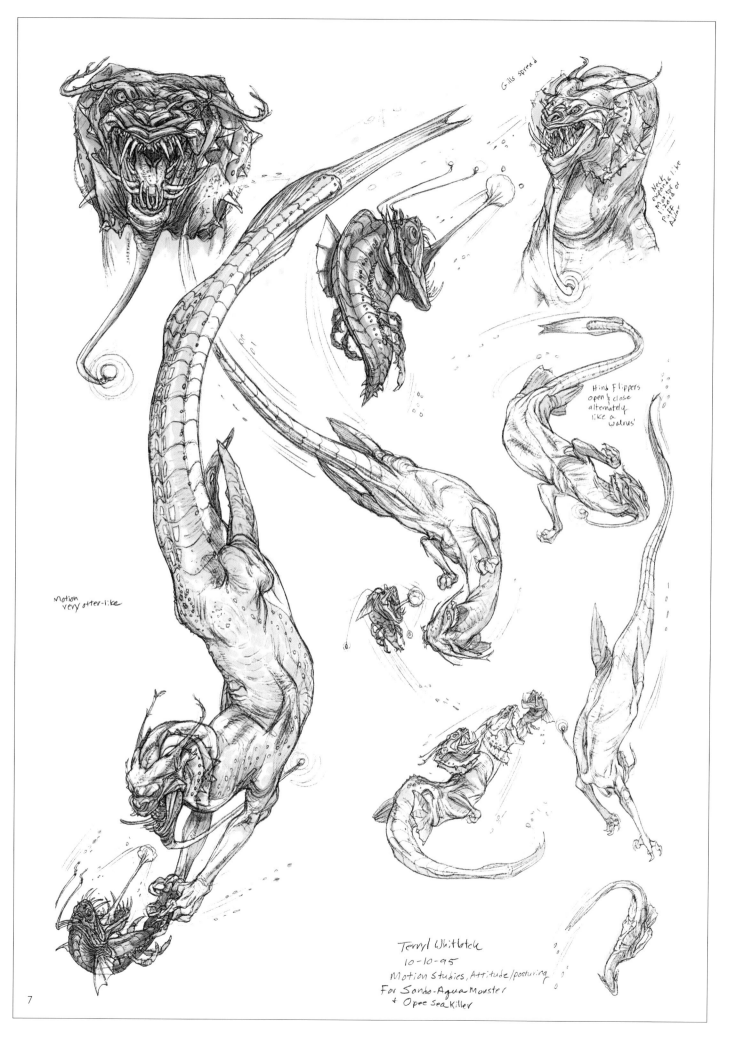

Gills spread

Neck expands like mantle like Puff Adder

Hind Flippers open & close alternately like a walrus'

Motion very otter-like

Terryl Whitlatch
10-10-95
Motion Studies, Attitude/posturing
For Sando-Aqua Monster
+ Opee Sea Killer

7

Sando aqua monster
1, 2 Terryl Whitlatch
3 Doug Chiang
4 Robert Barnes

Terryl Whitlatch

1

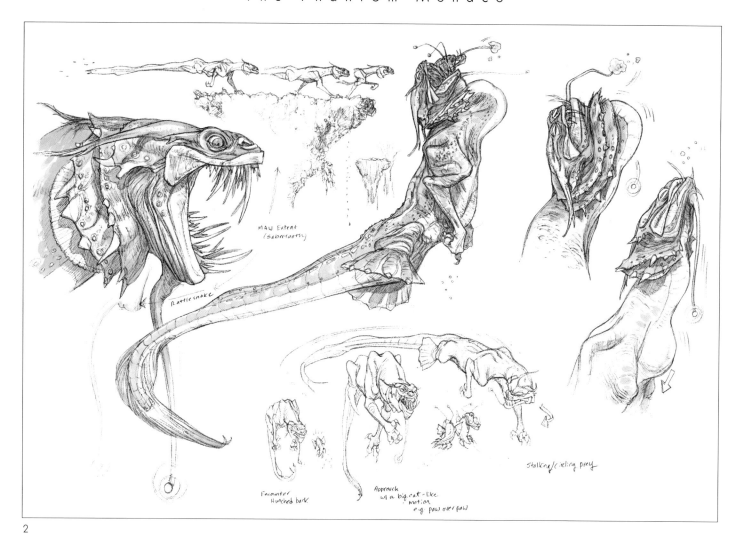

2

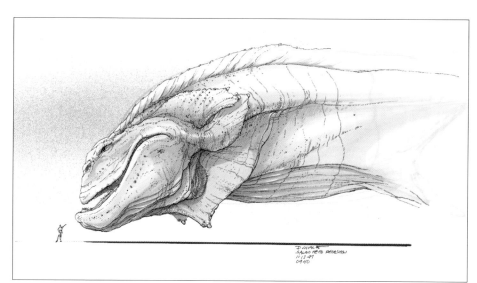

3

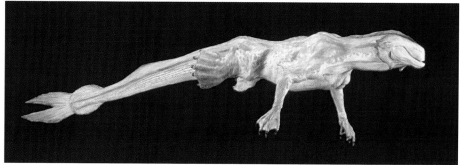

4

Attacking the opee sea killer, conceptual design (1)

Intermediate conceptual designs and motion studies (2):
Whitlatch wanted the sando to differ completely from the stereotypical sea monster, so she drew it as a "sea panther." Although the sando does have gills at this stage, much of its anatomy was drawn from tigers and otters. Whitlatch also wanted it to appear more intelligent than the colo and the opee.

Head and neck, revised conceptual design (3):
As animation began on the sando, Lucas felt it still wasn't quite large enough, so Chiang magnified and altered it still further, making it terrifyingly huge, and the head more whalelike.

Sculpey concept maquette (4):
Ultimately, the sando's blue coloring was dropped in favor of a "Moby Dick" look, borrowing from narwhale and beluga coloration.

1

2

3

Gungan beasts of burden and swamp creatures

1–3 Terryl Whitlatch

Early in the development of the story, the citizens of Theed were to have more contact with the Gungans and the creatures of the swamp. Thus, Padmé was to have her own swamp "horse" (1).

69

Swamp creatures
1—8 Terryl Whitlatch

Nuna, orthographics:
The nuna, or "swamp turkey" (1), is the galactic equivalent of the rat—they turn up everywhere. Although native to the swamps of Naboo, they also skitter about such far-flung

2

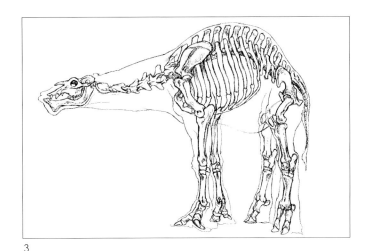

3

places as Jabba the Hutt's viewing box at the Boonta Eve Podrace on Tatooine. Whitlatch borrowed the nuna's unusual spot pattern from large, predatory cats.

Falumpaset, coloration and skeleton, conceptual designs (2,3):
The falumpaset's coloring is based on that of the Appaloosa horse.

Ikopi, conceptual design (4):
The ikopi was inspired by a North African/Saharan gazelle, with a few giraffelike characteristics added to the mix.

Peko-peko, early conceptual painting and color orthographic study (5, 7):
Whitlatch created an entire fictional ecosystem for Naboo, as well as a specific niche for each species. She noted, "the peko-peko is a strong-flying, arboreal repto-avian, with habits similar to the macaws of earth. It eats all sorts of vegetable matter, and is partial to large, hard-shelled nuts and fruits."

4

5

6

7

8

T. WHITLATCH '95

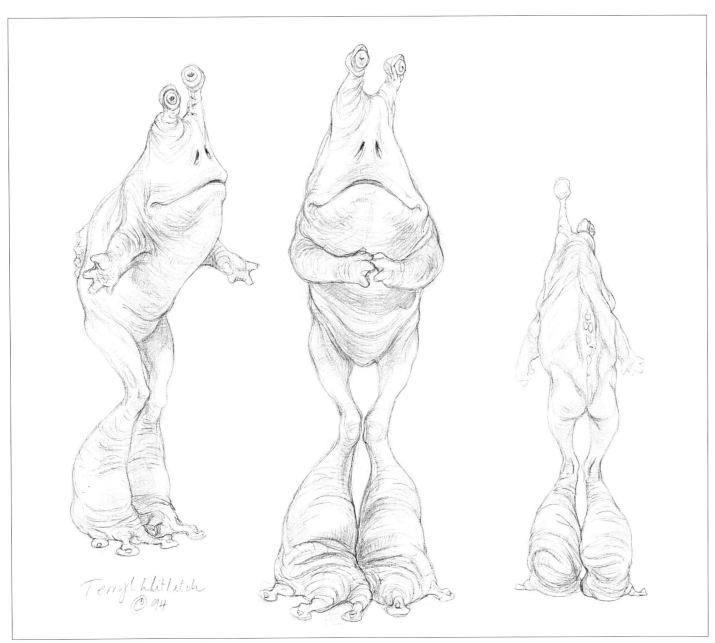

1

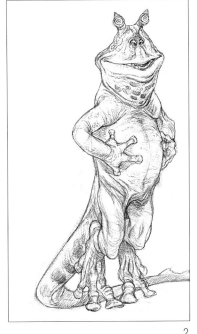

2

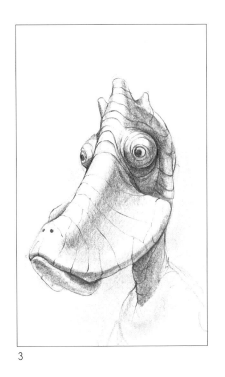

3

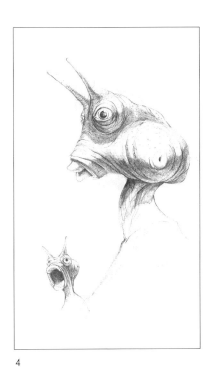

4

D.CHIANG '95

5

Gungans/Jar Jar Binks conceptual designs and painting
1, 2, 6, 7 Terryl Whitlatch
3–5 Doug Chiang

While taking a short break from her work, Whitlatch decided to draw a silly, frog/sluglike creature (1). George happened to notice it and found it consistent with his ideas for Jar Jar and the Gungans.

Jar Jar took several evolutionary sidesteps — growing a long prehensile tail (2, 6), as well as delving a bit into the seahorse (3), snail (4), and platypus characteristics (5).

Lucas felt that this intermediate design (7) was the first portrait to truly capture the essence of Jar Jar's screwball personality. Jar Jar is leaning on a Gungan "dog" named Blarf—a recurring character in Whitlatch's sketches, based on a real-life boxer dog named Abigail.

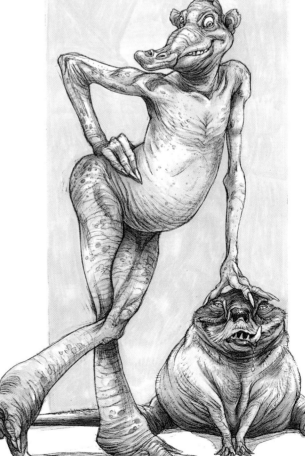

6

7

Gungans/Jar Jar Binks

1, 9 Terryl Whitlatch
2–6 Tony McVey
7 Iain McCaig
8 Tony Wright

Intermediate conceptual designs and movement studies (1, 9)

Intermediate Sculpey and cast resin conceptual models (2–6)

Gungan with clothing, intermediate conceptual design (7)

Male and female Gungans and skin texture, intermediate conceptual design (8)

1

2

3

4

5

6

7

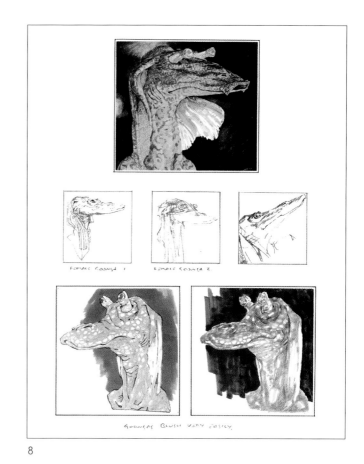

8

GOONGAS BLUSH VERY EASILY

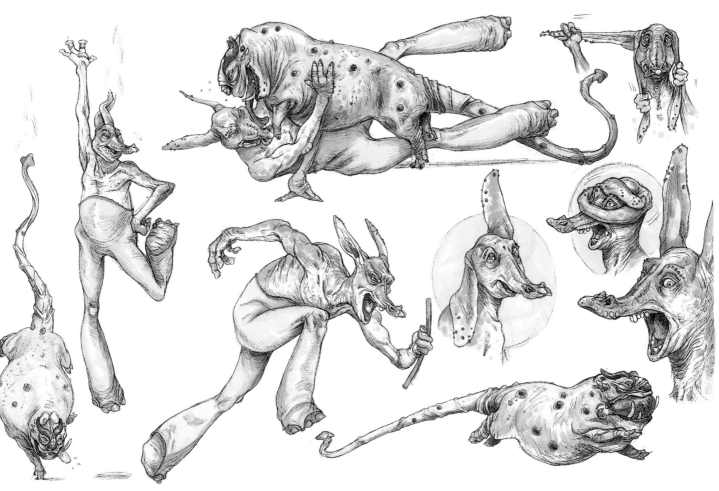

9

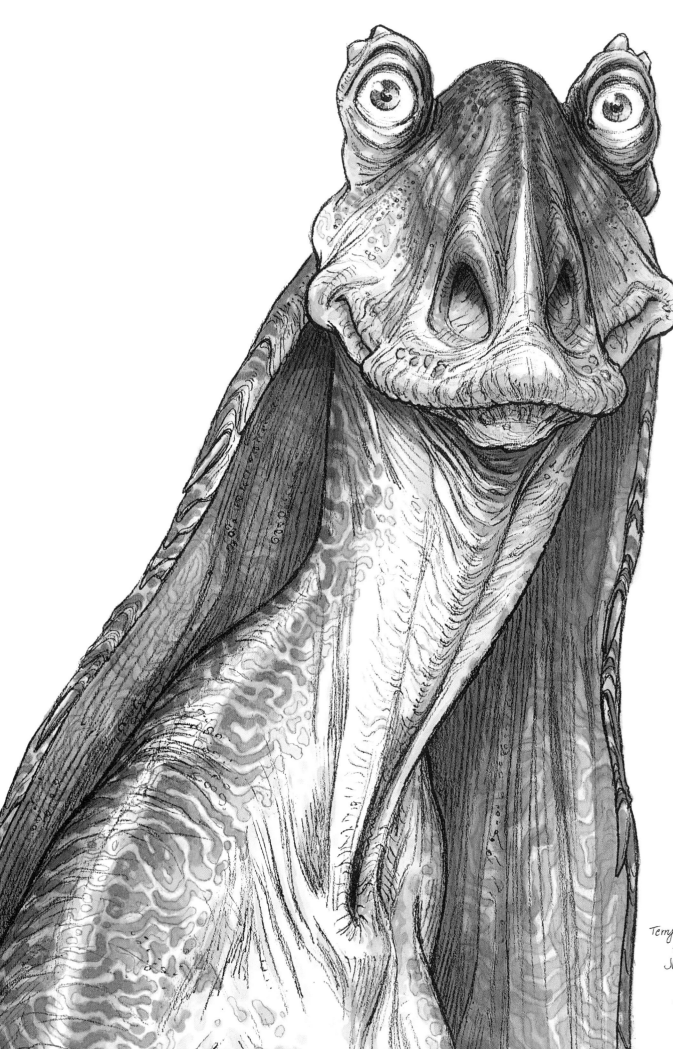

Terryl Whitlatch
8-1-96
JAR JAR BINX

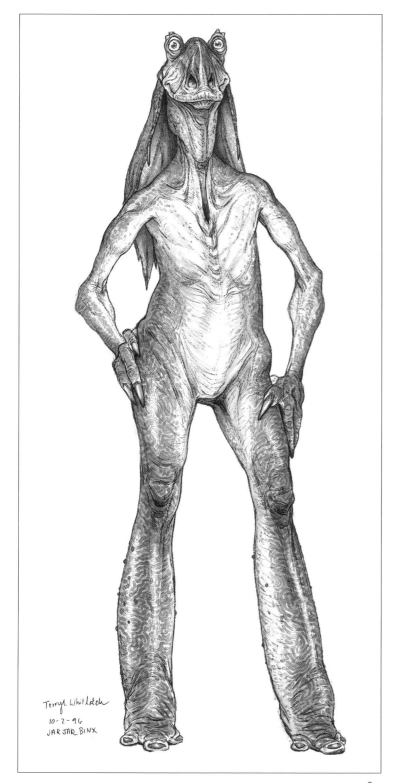

2

4

5

3

6

Jar Jar Binks

1, 2, 4–6 Terryl Whitlatch
3 Iain McCaig

Final conceptual design (1, 2)

Costume, conceptual design (3)

Gungan color variations, conceptual designs (4–6)

Jar Jar Binks, expression studies
Iain McCaig

1

2

3

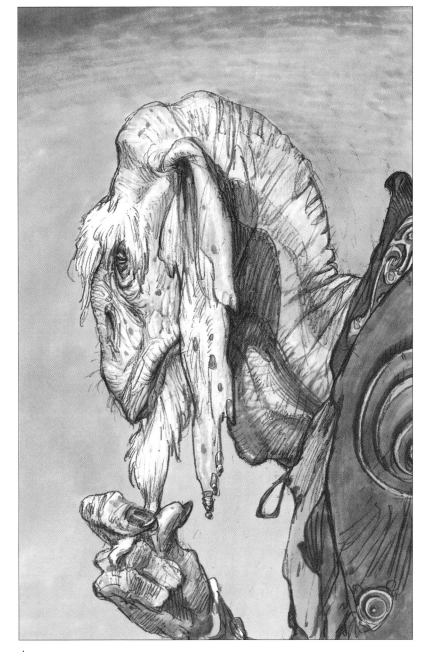

4

5

Boss Nass/Gungans

1, 2 Terryl Whitlatch
4, 9 Iain McCaig
3, 5 Edwin Natividad
6, 8 Doug Chiang
7 Doug Chiang/Edwin Natividad

Boss Nass, conceptual designs (1, 3, 5)

Gungan citizens of various ages with clothing, intermediate conceptual designs (2, 4)

Boss Nass victory parade saddle and mount, conceptual design (6)

Boss Nass with council members, story-board panel (7) and conceptual design (9)

Queen Amidala and Boss Nass forge their alliance. Production painting (8)

6

7

8

9

1

Creature Cavalry

1–5 Doug Chiang

Naboo air and ground patrols, production painting and conceptual designs (1, 2, 5):
Initially the end battle was going to involve Naboo cavalry fighting alongside the Gungan warriors, so Chiang gave the Naboo military similar creature mounts.

Gungan heavy cavalry, early fambaa and mounted weaponry designs:
At this point in production, Lucas hadn't yet decided that the drums shown here (3, 4) would become shield generators, so Chiang designed some to be sonic cannons (3), and some to be armored personnel carriers (4).

2

D.CHIANG '95

3

4

5

1

Kaadu

1, 2 Doug Chiang
3, 4 Terryl Whitlatch

Gungan cavalry, production painting (1)

Gungan cavalry creatures, early conceptual designs:
In late 1995, Lucas decided to put a version of the eopie (the beast of burden created for Tatooine), on Naboo, and give it to the Gungans. Chiang thus transformed the eopie into the kaadu (2). An amphibious animal, the kaadu is much larger and faster than the eopie, and is the perfect battle steed.

Kaadu, conceptual paintings:
Lucas didn't want the kaadu to look too dinosaurlike, so he encouraged Terry Whitlatch to give the kaadu's skin more fishlike hues and textures, along with some birdlike coloration (3, 4).

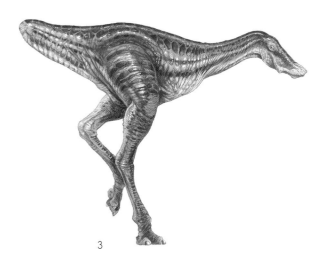

3

D.CHIANG
GOONGA CAVALRY
12·14·95
0502

2

4

1

2

3

4

Cavalry beasts
1–5 Terryl Whitlatch
6 Evan Pontoriero

Early conceptual designs (1, 4)

Fambaa, finished conceptual design and animation cycle:
Once the four-legged version of the fambaa was approved (2), Whitlatch created these animation cycles to show the artists at ILM how the fambaa should walk (3).

Gungan cavalry charge, conceptual design (5)

Droid/Gungan battle, animatic frame (6)

5

6

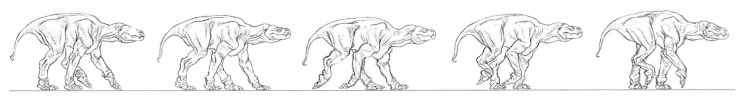

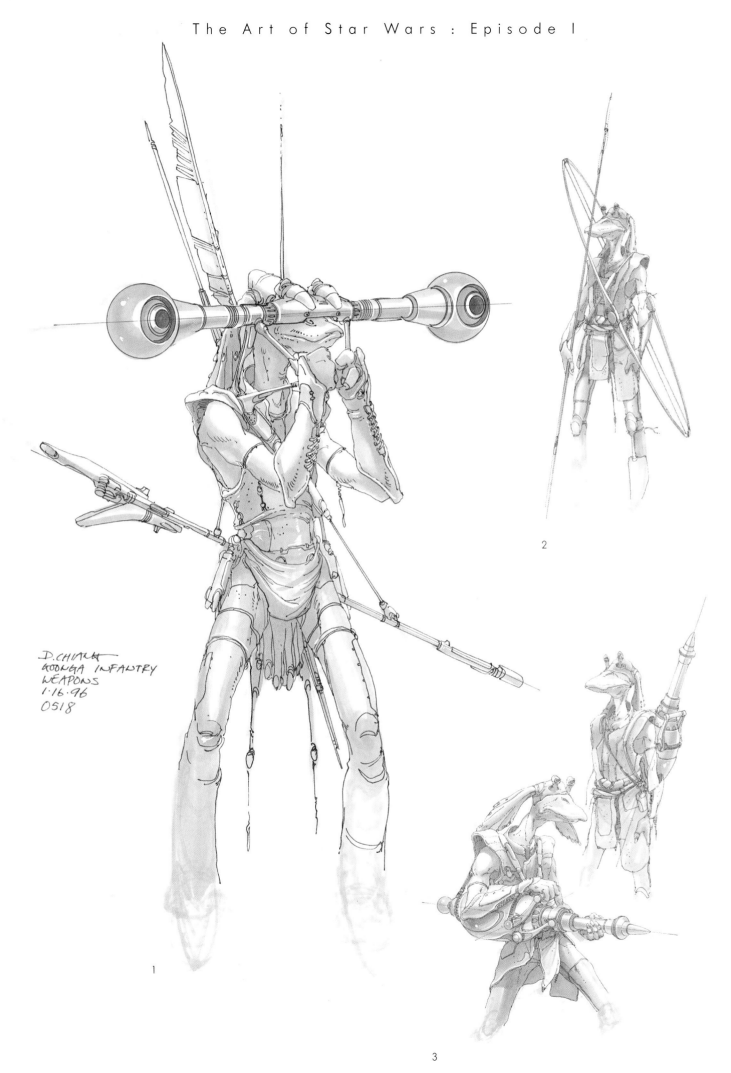

D.CHIARET
GOONGA INFANTRY
WEAPONS
1·16·96
0518

1

2

3

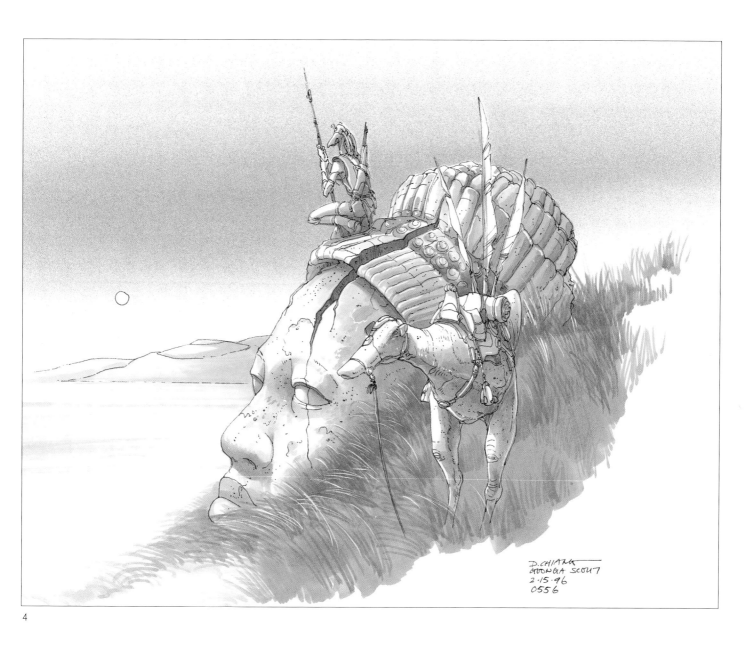

4

Gungan military
1–5 Doug Chiang

Gungan with "farseein" field binoculars, conceptual design (1)

Infantry weapons and costumes, conceptual designs (2, 3)

Scout atop sacred statue, conceptual design (4):
A Gungan scout stands watch atop a sacred ruin. These giant sculpted heads were originally created for Naboo, then, for a time, were moved to Tatooine to serve as obstacles in the Podrace, only to be finally moved back to Naboo.

Cavalry, production painting (5)

5

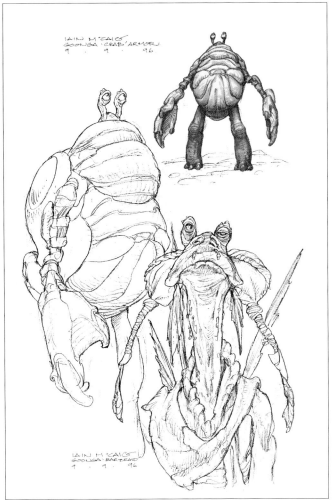

1

Gungan armor, conceptual designs
1–5, 8 Iain McCaig
6, 7 Edwin Natividad

For a short period of time, crab-shell armor was considered for the Gungans (1). Ultimately, however, leather became the material of choice (6, 7), not only because the Gungans are a "primitive" species, but also because it is easier to animate. By dressing the Gungans in tight-fitting leather and metal, the digital artists didn't have to animate the shifting and creasing that is characteristic of lighter materials.

2

3

4

5

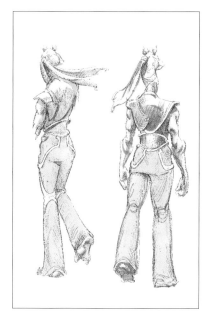

6

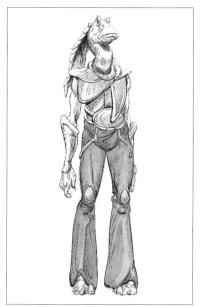

7

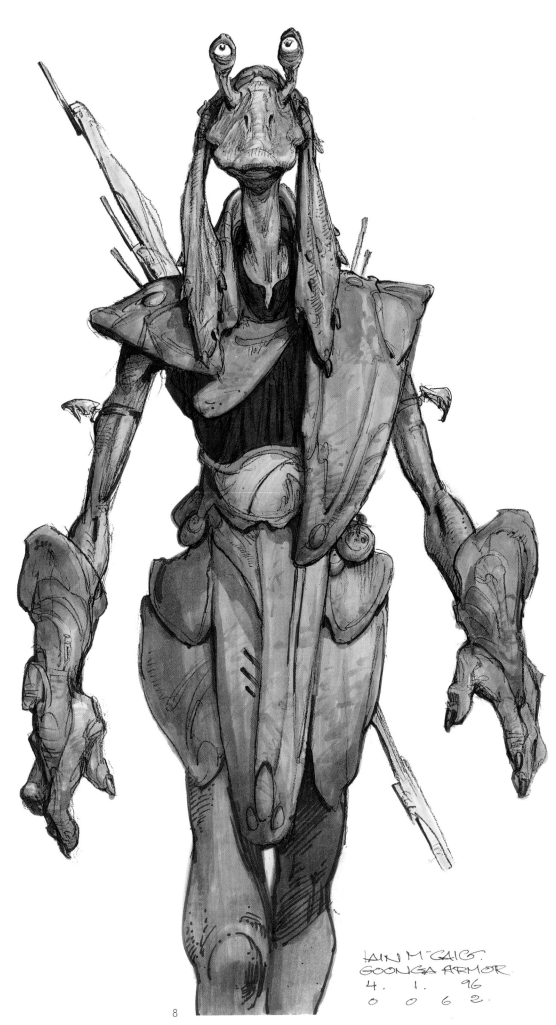

8

IAIN M°CAIG.
GOONGA ARMOR
4. 1. 96
0 0 6 2.

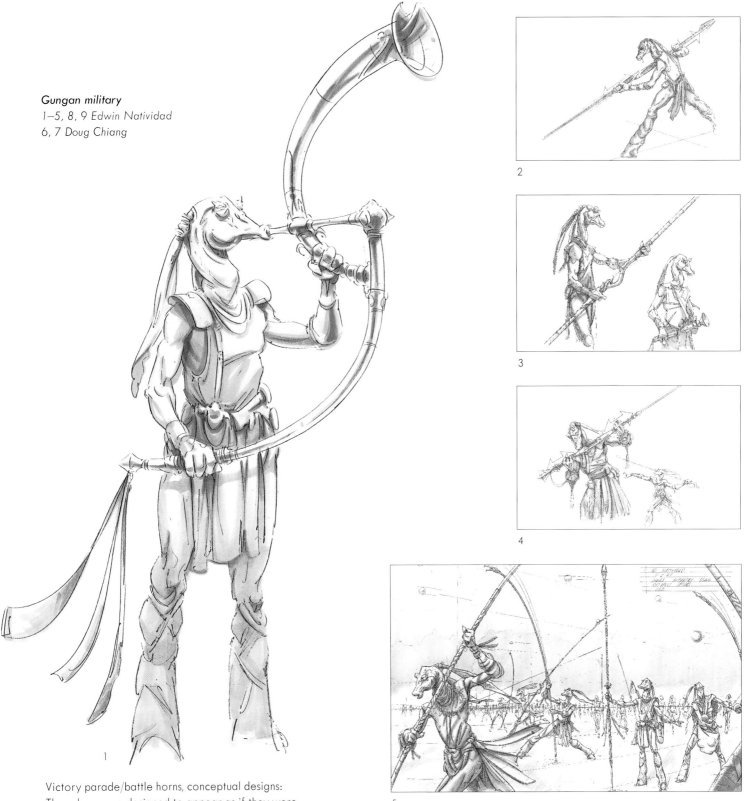

Gungan military
1–5, 8, 9 Edwin Natividad
6, 7 Doug Chiang

1

2

3

4

5

Victory parade/battle horns, conceptual designs:
These horns are designed to appear as if they were
organically grown—hence the calcium deposit/
seashell look (1).

Infantry weapons and costumes, conceptual designs
(2–5):
A lot of the look of Gungan weaponry was drawn
from aboriginal cultures, particularly Australian and
African, but was supplemented with alien forms such
as energy balls.

Battle wagon with falumpaset, final conceptual
design (6)

The Gungan army emerges from the swamp.
Production painting (7)

Energy cannon, initial and final conceptual designs:
Lucas felt the original version (8) of the Gungan
energy cannon was too literal; it looked like it could
have existed in medieval Europe. He therefore
asked Natividad to sketch the second version, an
exotic, asymmetric design more in keeping with the
Gungan aesthetic (9).

6

7

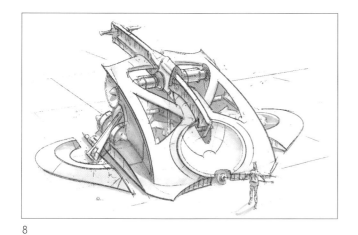

8

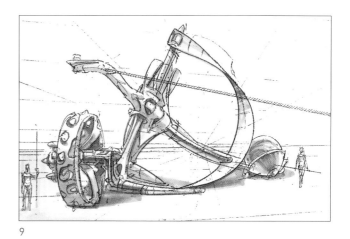

9

1

Droid/Gungan battle
1 Doug Chiang
2 Iain McCaig

AAT pursuing a Gungan cavalryman, production painting (1)

STAPs attacking a Gungan rider, storyboard (2)

2

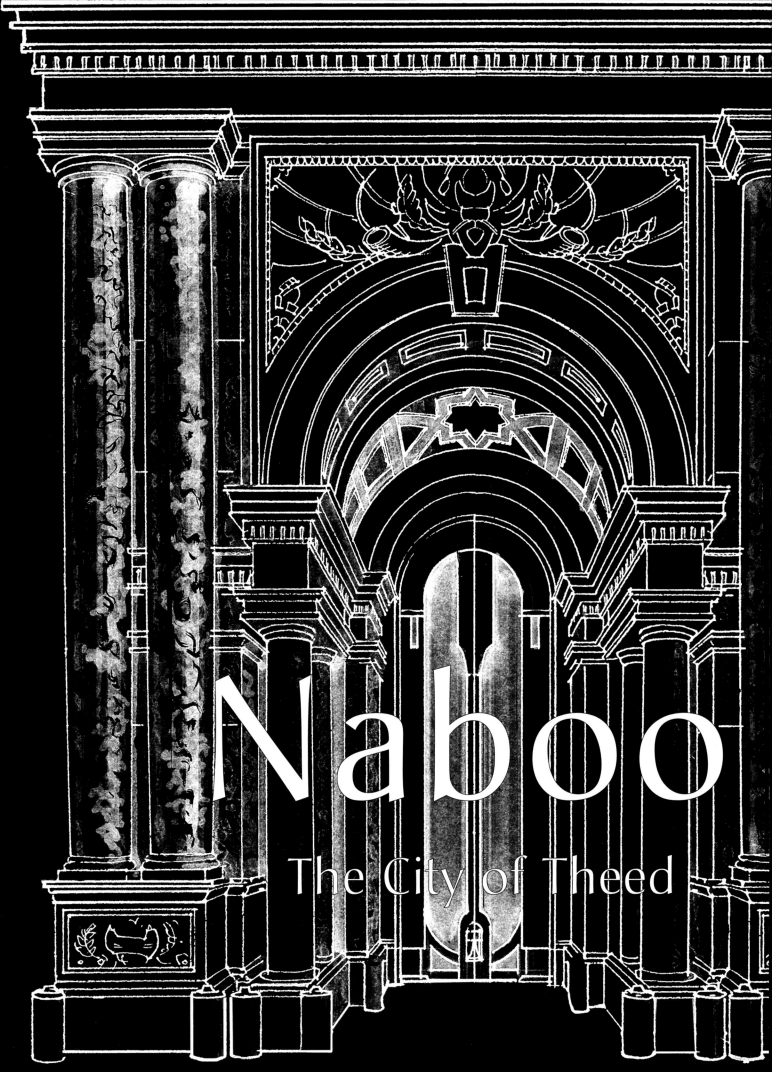

Naboo

The City of Theed

Under George Lucas' direction, the Naboo capital, Theed, gradually evolved into a paradise of a city, filled with fragrant, flourishing gardens and swiftly flowing rivers. Months were spent studying Mediterranean architecture—Moorish, Italian, Moroccan, and Turkish—and eventually the desired blend was achieved. Various cultural influences were merged to create a timeless, eclectic look. Working with producer Rick McCallum, London-based production designer Gavin Bocquet was then assigned the task of searching the Old World for a building that could match the look of Theed, and become its palace.

Fifteen miles north of Naples, Italy, lies the town of Caserta, home of the Palazzo Reale, the palace of the Bourbon kings. Built to emulate Versailles, it is famous for its marbled corridors, magnificent sculptures, and sweeping grand staircase. In July of 1997, it also became the palace of Queen Amidala.

The Palazzo Reale fit in seamlessly with the art department's design work. A baroque-rococo palace built in 1752, its grand interior meshed quite nicely with Theed's energetic strength and splendor, as well as its light sense of beauty and amiability. Once Caserta was settled upon as the location most consistent with the look of Theed, the art department drafted up designs that would digitally modify the interior of the Palazzo Reale, so it would fit Lucas' conception of the Queen's palace.

Next the artists had to address a problem presented by the exterior. Amidala's palace needed to symbolize the philosophy of the Naboo, and so it had to be a building that wouldn't mar the natural beauty of the landscape, but would actually improve upon it. Part of the answer was found close to home in the form of Marin County's Civic Center, a striking complex of dome-covered, aqueductlike buildings nestled in the hills above California's Highway 101.

Further inspiration came from the Blue Mosque—also known as Sultan Ahmet Mosque—one of Istanbul's more prominent houses of worship. Known for its series of multi-sized domes and its six towering minarets, the Blue Mosque is a startlingly fanciful building, remarkable for its sense of composition and symmetry.

Thus, the art department incorporated elements of the Blue Mosque, along with an eclectic mix of Venetian architecture, into the palace and the rest of Theed's architecture. Buildings such as the starfighter hangar, the generator station, and the funeral rotunda quickly fell into place.

Following suit, Theed's culture began to take shape. Again Lucas pursued an art nouveau sensibility. The philosophy of art nouveau developed in part as a reaction to the craftless, bulk manufacturing championed by turn-of-the-twentieth-century industrialists. As such, it provided a perfect balance to the mechanized look of the Trade Federation.

However, since the people of Naboo weren't as reclusive as the amphibious Gungans, they would be members of the Galactic Republic and have access to its advanced technology. Lucas and his team had to figure out a way to convey sophisticated machinery in art nouveau terms. The solution was to make Theed's technology a sort of mirror of Otoh Gunga's biology: the Gungans would have organically-based machinery, and the Naboo would have actual machinery that appeared organic.

With this style in mind, the art department began implementing an elegant, overtly handcrafted look. Everything was to be smooth and curvilinear, with touches of chrome thrown in to provide a unique stylistic sense; a style McCaig dubbed "space nouveau." However, because the Naboo had commercial ties with the rest of the Republic, examples of non-native technology would not be uncommon, such as R2-D2 and the other astromech droids seen on Queen Amidala's starship.

As for Naboo clothing and personal accessories, Lucas wanted the costumes to be flowing and diaphanous and made from elegant, ethereal fabrics. According to the director, the people of Theed were to be dressed in the "clothing of paradise," so concept artist Iain McCaig and costume designer Trisha Biggar drew heavily on the works of the Pre-Raphaelites, with the occasional World War I flight costume, and a bit more art nouveau thrown in for good measure. As for Queen Amidala, her costumes were based on Tibetan and Mongolian ceremonial vestments.

The end result was a serene, pacifistic society that merged detailed craftsmanship with advanced technology. By combining different time periods and schools of design, the art department made Theed into a romantic, retro-futuristic civilization that would ultimately have to withstand the assault of the Trade Federation.

1

2

Theed Palace
1 Doug Chiang
2 Edwin Natividad
3 Jay Shuster
4 Brian Flora

Production painting and storyboards (1–3):
Influenced by Frank Lloyd Wright's Marin County Civic Center and Istanbul's Blue Mosque, the Theed palace was designed to exist in harmony with its natural surroundings.

Matte painting (4)

Pages 96–97: Theed Palace facade, final conceptual design
Kurt Kaufman

3

4

1

Theed Palace and urban architecture
1 Kurt Kaufman
2, 3 Doug Chiang
4 Ellen Lee

Facade, final conceptual design (1)

Theed street, conceptual design (2, 3):
To create Theed's "timeless look," Chiang mixed together an unusual blend of high-tech streetlamps and wall sconces with classic, Venetian-style architecture.

City plan, foam core conceptual model (4)

2

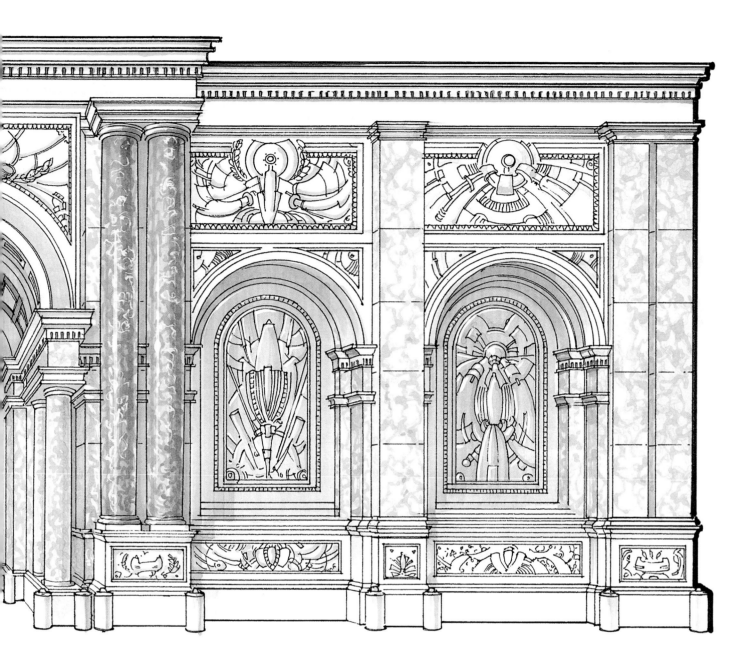

3

4

Theed Palace exteriors and interiors
1, 3–11 Edwin Natividad
2 Kurt Kaufman

Exterior statues, conceptual designs (1, 3–6):
Designed to look as if made of marble and approximately one hundred feet tall, these figures are characters from Theed mythology.

Queen Amidala's throne and table, conceptual and orthographic designs:
Throne designs were made to be low and wide to allow for nice backlighting. They were also designed to emphasize the unique silhouette created by the Queen's costume (7–9, 11). For

7

the table, Natividad played with different shapes (7–10) and materials (such as wood, marble, and metal) to create a configuration that would best match the Palazzo Reale. He finally settled upon a sophisticated, yet aggressive, conical shape (7, 10).

Exterior, matte painting (2)

10

8

9

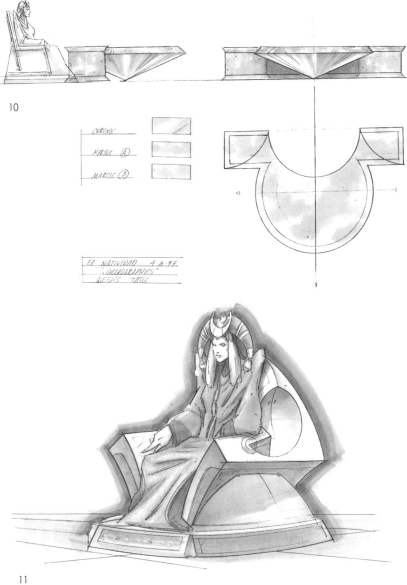

11

1

2

3

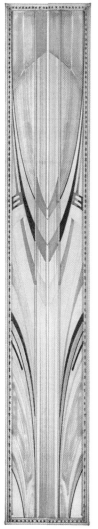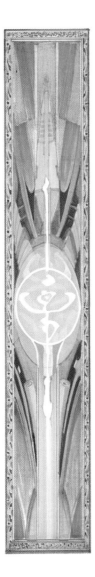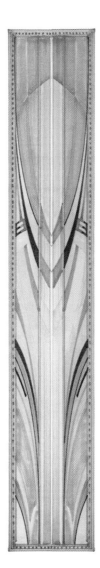

4

Victory parade
1–3 Doug Chiang
4 Kurt Kaufman

This early drawing (1) of the victory parade
included an air whale flyby—later cut due to
the elimination of the air whales (2). In another
sketch (3), Boss Nass is carried to the Theed
palace on a litter.

Theed Palace parade banners, conceptual
designs (4)

1

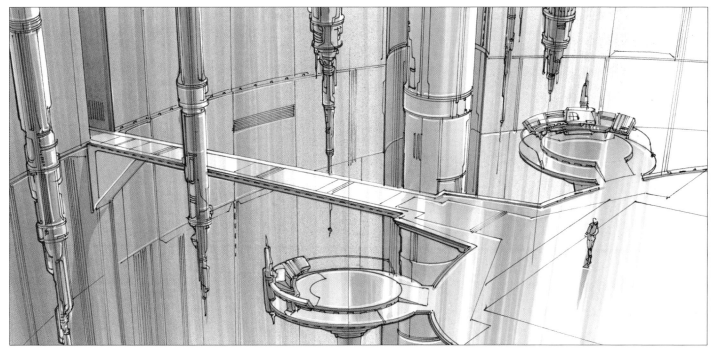

2

3

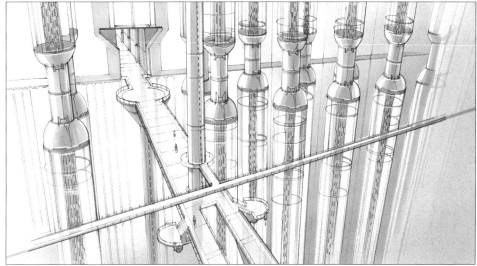

4

5

Generator complex

1, 2, 4 Doug Chiang
3 Jay Shuster
5 Kurt Kaufman

Theed exterior, conceptual design (1)

First and second rooms, conceptual designs (2, 4):
While Theed's exteriors are designed to enhance their natural surroundings, the interior of the generator station is an expansive, artificial environment. Chiang thought of it as an energy well, with a few touches of Cloud City thrown in, such as the thin catwalks extending out into a vast, open space.
Entrance, interior, conceptual design (3)

Interior wall paneling, conceptual designs (5)

IAIN M^cCAIG.
QUEEN (HAIR)

1

2

3

5

6

4

7

Queen Amidala's costumes, conceptual designs
1–8 Iain McCaig

Remembering the response to Princess Leia's hairdo, Lucas decided to be even more outrageous this time around and encouraged McCaig to be particularly outlandish in his designs (1–4).

Before Amidala's species or general look had been decided on, McCaig experimented a little (5, 6).

During the evolution of Queen Amidala's Senate costume, the Mongolian hairstyle in this first sketch (7) was kept; the large, muff sleeves were toned down (8).

8

1

2

3

*Amidala/Padmé costumes,
conceptual designs*
1–9 Iain McCaig

As the Queen's battle dress developed, the belly straps from the initial sketch (1) were dropped for the finished design (5), because in real life they would be awkward and uncomfortable. According to McCaig, when he decided to incorporate some lanterns into the hem of Amidala's palace dress, Lucas rolled his eyes and made McCaig draw up schematics of how it would actually work. McCaig rose to the occasion, and the dress was ultimately approved (2).

4

5

6

7

8

9

In an early, art nouveau version of the Queen's victory parade costume inspired by Alphonse Mucha (3), she is wearing a wide fan on her back.

The design process was at times frustrating, and in one instance, McCaig began angrily scribbling over his work. Just as he was about to crumple up the paper and throw it away, he realized he liked the pattern he subconsiously had doodled. Lucas liked it as well, and ultimately, the costume was worn by Sabé, the Queen's decoy (4).

In *A New Hope*, Lucas had wanted to give Princess Leia a Hopi Indian hairstyle much like the ones seen on Padmé (9). Unsure as to whether or not Lucas would want a variant of Leia's cinnamon bun, however, McCaig tried longer, more ornamental, and art nouveau variations (6–8).

2

3   4

Padmé/handmaiden hair and costume, conceptual designs
1–7 Iain McCaig

While Amidala wore her hair up, with heavy head ornaments, McCaig gave the handmaidens a lighter look. Their hairstyles (1) were less elaborate and had a more Pre-Raphaelite/art nouveau flavor.

1

Since Naboo costumes had an element of disguise to them, particularly in the case of the Queen, McCaig tried to design clothing that would obscure any hints of size, shape, or age (1, 3, 4, 7).

5

6   7

1

2

3

IAIN M°CAIG
NABOO MAN
2 . 10 . 97

4

5

Naboo scientist and Royal Security Force costumes, conceptual designs
1, 2, 4–6 Iain McCaig
3 Trisha Biggar/costume department

Iain McCaig: "A big problem with a soft, peaceful, Pre-Raphaelite world like Naboo was figuring out how to make the men look tough. Do you give them holsters, like this palace guard (1)? Boots? What effect do leggings have on the costume of this Naboo scientist, based on conceptual researcher David Craig (2)? Do you just mush together old sci-fi serials and cowboy westerns (4)? Throw in some leather armor (6)? For the pilots (7), I was inspired by World War I combat fliers. And finally, for helmets and hats (5), I studied pith and military helmets."

Costume helmet (3)

6

7

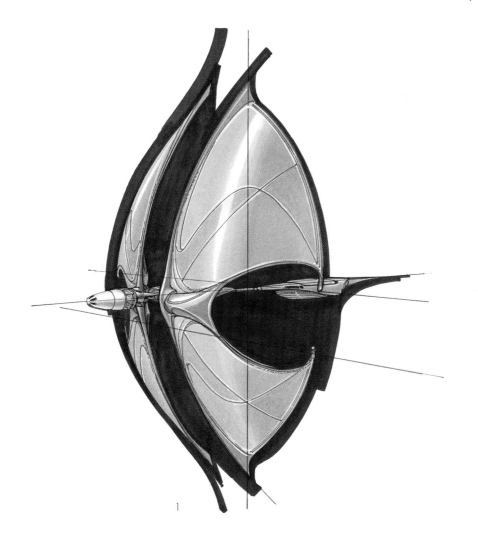

Queen Amidala's J-type 327 Nubian starship, conceptual designs
1–8 Doug Chiang

Originally the Queen's ship was to be a yacht powered by a solar sail (1–3). When the ship needed to go into hyperspace, the sail would fold up, and the ship would rocket off. One version (1) came very close to being the final design, until Lucas decided he wanted a sleek, chrome ship. Chiang then generated the earliest chrome version (5), inspired by 1950s-style automobile hood ornaments. The next two chrome versions (6, 7) began to draw on real-world supersonic aircraft, but were not regal enough. Chiang also tried an alternate, squid-like configuration (4) to play up the watery nature of Naboo, but Lucas didn't go for it. Finally, after further study, Chiang came up with the finished design (8).

1

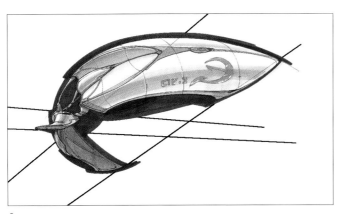

2

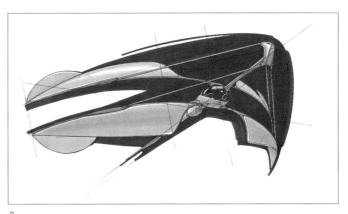

3

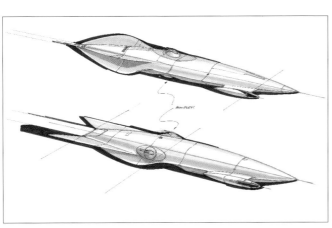

4

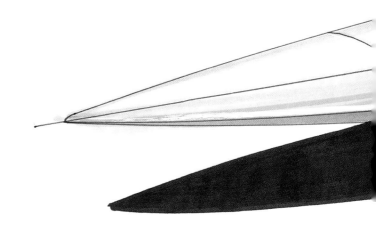

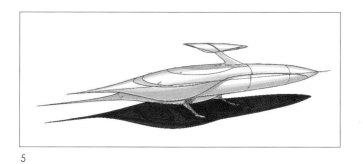

5

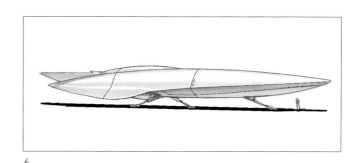

6

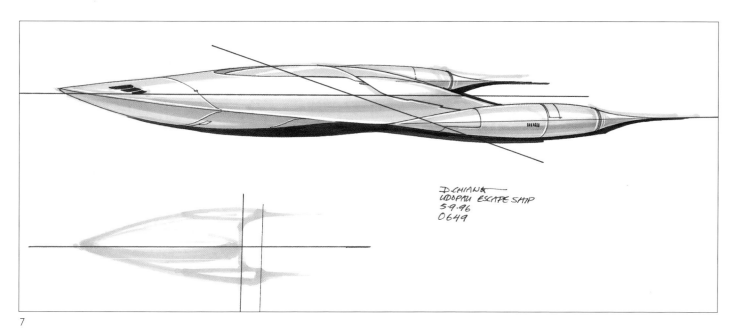

D. CHIANG
UDOPAU ESCAPE SHIP
5.9.96
O649

7

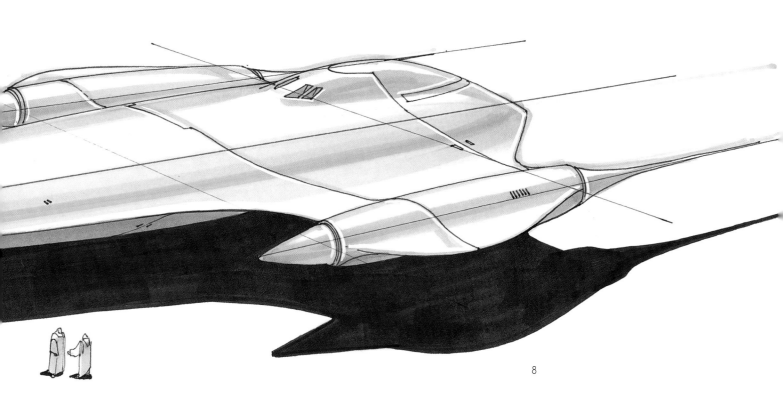

8

1

Queen Amidala's J-type 327 Nubian starship
1—4 Doug Chiang

In the production painting for the Jedi battle in
the desert(1), Qui-Gon and Darth Maul duel
alongside the Queen's ship.

Hatch and landing gear, conceptual designs
(2—4)

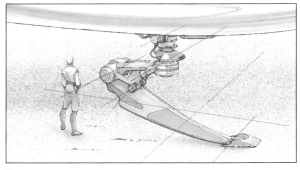

2

D. CHIANG

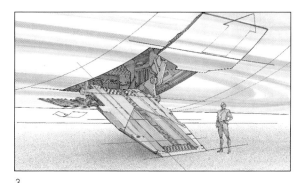

3

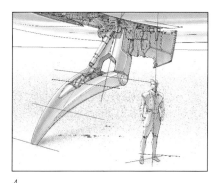

4

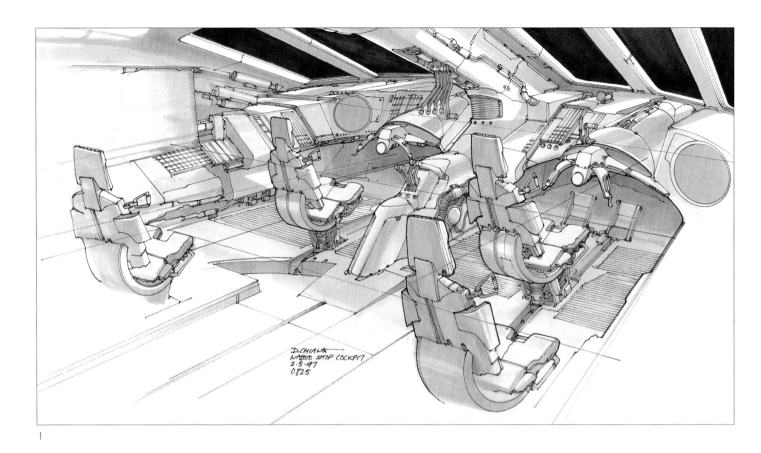

1

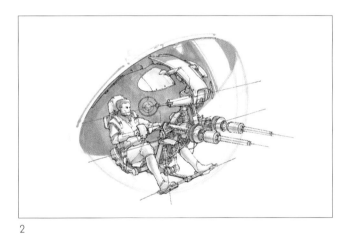

2

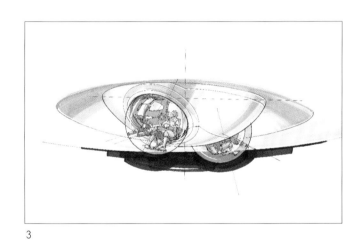

3

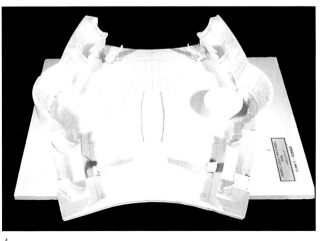

4

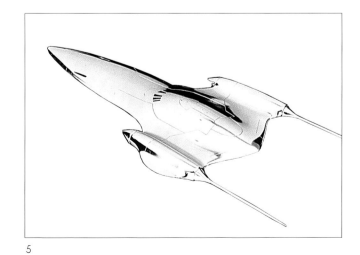

5

6

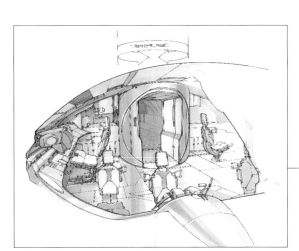

7

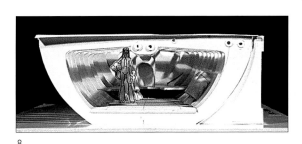

8

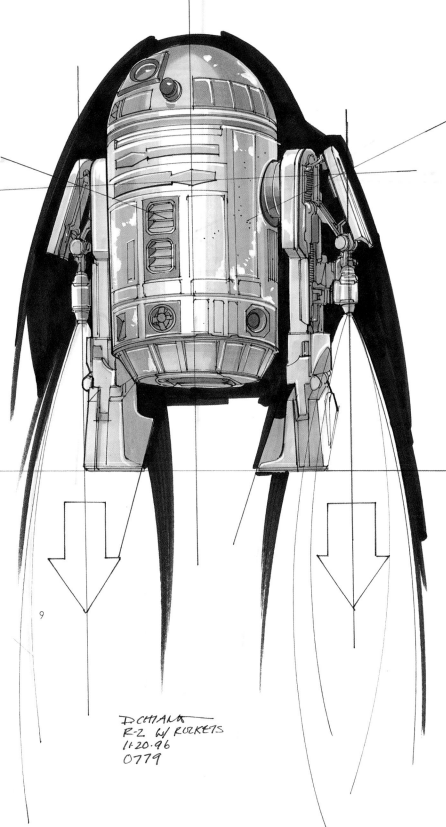

9

Queen Amidala's J-type 327 Nubian starship
1–3, 6, 7, 9 Doug Chiang
4, 8 Gavin Bocquet/production design team
5 John Goodson

Cockpit interiors, conceptual designs (1, 7)

Gunner turrets, conceptual designs (2, 3):
At one point, the Queen's ship was to be armed and Qui-Gon and Obi-Wan were to use these turrets to fight off the starfighter droids. These were eliminated when Lucas decided to make the Queen's vessel a ship of peace.

Main hold and droid hold, conceptual card models (4, 8)

Conceptual model (5)

R2-D2, conceptual designs:
Lucas wanted R2-D2 to be able to do more in this film, so here we see Artoo in full-exploded capacity, with arms out and head raised (6). Artoo was also to be outfitted with rockets so that he could fly over obstacles (9).

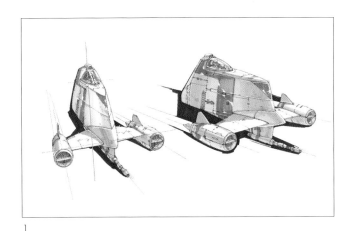

1

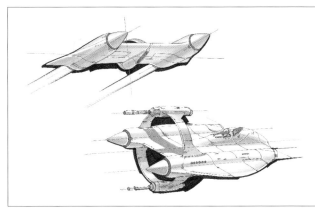

2

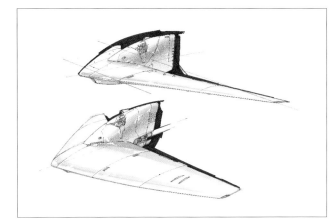

4

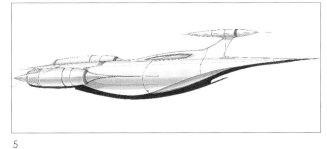

5

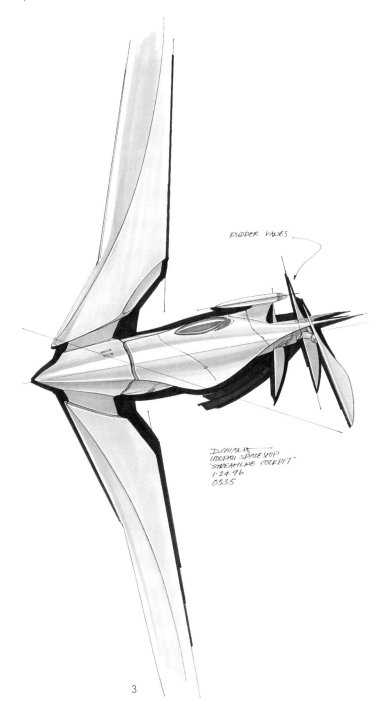

RUDDER VANES

D.CHIANG
UDOPAU SPACE SHIP
"STREAMLINE COCKPIT"
1·24·96
0535

3

Naboo Royal N-1 Starfighter, conceptual designs
1–7 Doug Chiang

At first the starfighter harkened back to the angular aesthetic of the original trilogy (1), but more rounded looks soon evolved (2), as well as a flying-wing style (4). At one point Lucas toyed with the idea of a ship with long, glider-type wings (3) that would pivot around the ship's central axis so that when it flew it formed a big vertical fin, but when it landed, the wings would be horizontal. Eventually, Lucas and Chiang decided the starfighter should be a smaller, fighter craft version of the Queen's ship, and the final version of the starfighter began to take shape (5). After a couple of experiments with the proportions, the design process nearly concluded with this sketch (6). All that remained was to remove the rocket launcher and detail the cockpit (7).

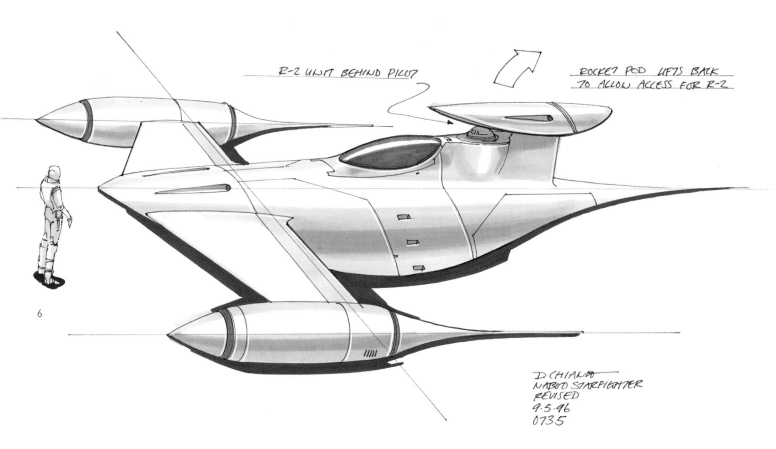

R-2 UNIT BEHIND PILOT

ROCKET POD LIFTS BACK
TO ALLOW ACCESS FOR R-2

D CHIANG
NABOO STARFIGHTER
REVISED
9·5·96
0735

6

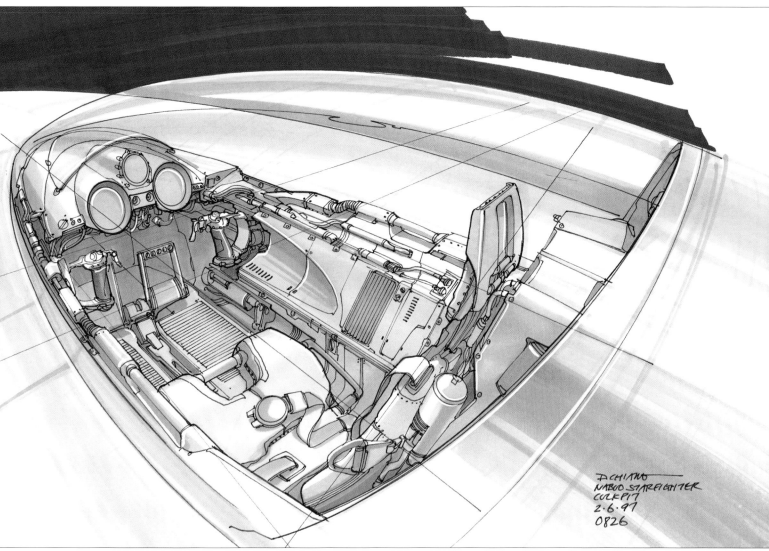

R-2 UNIT BEHIND PILOT

D CHIANG
NABOO STARFIGHTER
COCKPIT
2·6·97
0826

7

1

The N-1 Starfighter in action
1 Doug Chiang
2 Kevin Baillie

In an early rendition of the space battle (1), the since-deleted missile launcher is still on top of the N-1, and the Trade Federation starfighters are still saucer-shaped and droid-piloted. Also, the bridge of the Trade Federation battleship is back by the engines instead of being in the ball.

An N-1 streaks out of the Theed hangar. Animatic frame (2).

2

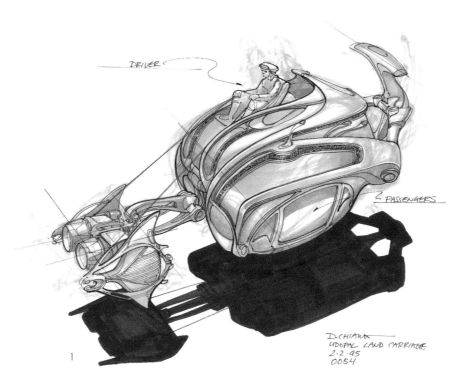

DRIVER

2 PASSENGERS

D. CHIANG
UDOPAL LAND CARRIAGE
2·2·95
0054

1

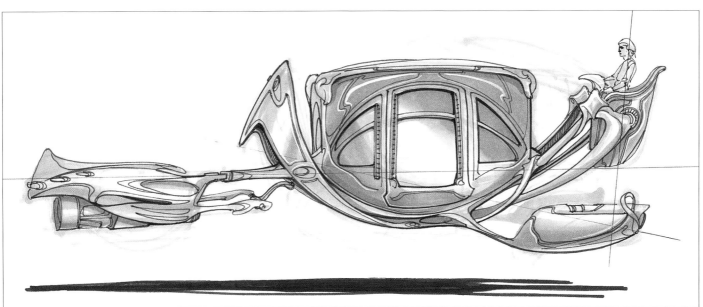

2

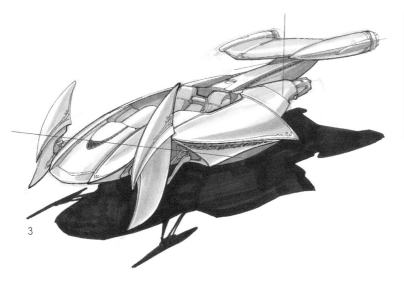

3

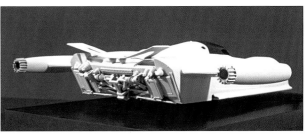

4

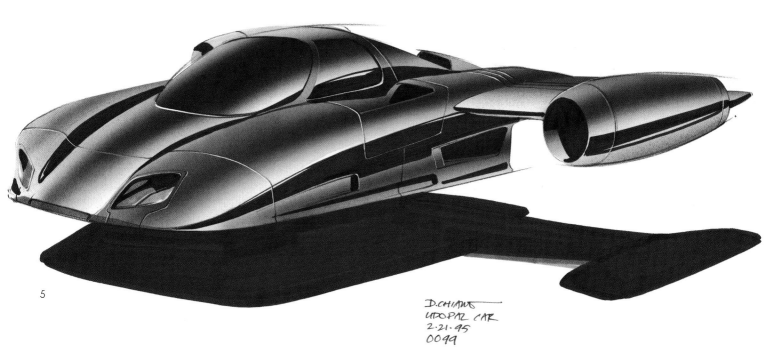

5

D.CHIANG
UTOPIA CAR
2·21·95
0099

6

7

8

9

Naboo land carriages and Flash speeders,
conceptual designs and model
1—3, 5—9 Doug Chiang
4 John Goodson

Prior to Lucas' establishing that the Naboo would employ landspeeder technology, Chiang designed a number of elegant, decorative land carriages (1, 2). Once Lucas introduced the landspeeder to Theed, Chiang attempted to apply some of the same aesthetic to speeder design (3), but wasn't quite satisfied with the results. Lucas soon decided that the Flash speeders should exhibit a Le Mans—style race car look (4—7).

Later in the production, Lucas decided to give the Naboo a larger, armed speeder, described as "a pick-up truck with guns," for which Chiang drew the sketches (8, 9).

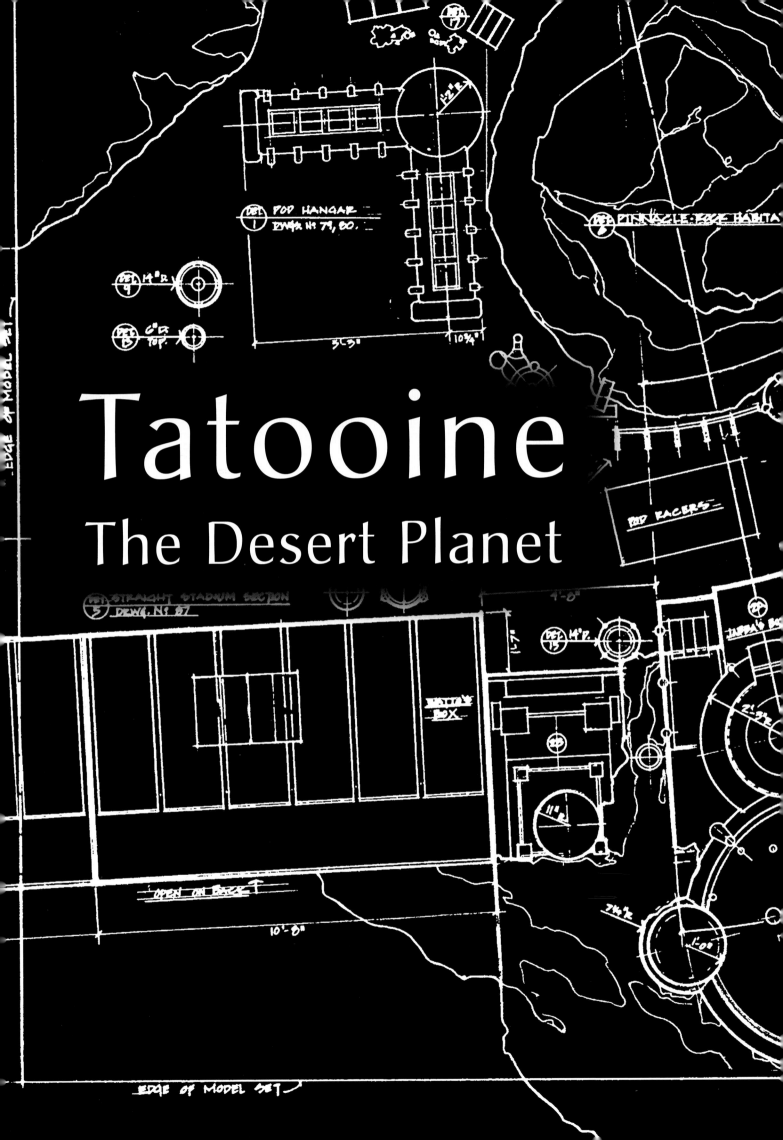

Tatooine
The Desert Planet

From the very earliest production paintings created by Ralph McQuarrie for *Star Wars: A New Hope* to the more recent work of Doug Chiang and Gavin Bocquet, Tatooine has always been depicted as the galactic equivalent of the Barbary Coast, a lawless world of gangsters and pirates. A scorching, twin-sunned planet, its soil is parched and barren, its air is searing to the lungs, and its landscape is blinding due to the stark, yellow sand. Because the climate is so exceedingly harsh, resources are scarce, and daily life is a constant struggle. To paraphrase Thucydides, on Tatooine the strong do as they will and the weak suffer as they must.

The architecture of Tatooine reflects two concerns—shelter from merciless heat and protection from merciless people. As in the original trilogy, the Tatooine scenes would be filmed in the North African nation of Tunisia, and Tunisian architecture was closely studied for the appropriate architectural features.

In *Star Wars: A New Hope*, Luke Skywalker's pit house was based on Berber troglodyte dwellings. Built by the Berber people of North Africa, troglodyte dwellings are underground homes which are nearly invisible from the surface, provide cool relief from the blazing heat of the day, and retain their warmth during the freezing night.

Early in the making of *The Phantom Menace*, Lucas proposed to expand on this idea and to create entire cityscapes built at the bottom of gigantic pits, with the outskirts of these cities reaching into the canyon walls, like the Anasazi Indian settlements of the American southwest. Neighboring cities would be connected via a series of artificial gorges. Although developmental sketches for such cities were created, it became clear early on that the creation of these sets, practical or digital, would be much too expensive and time consuming. However, a bit of this look was retained for the Podrace arena and Beggar's Canyon.

Lucas decided instead to make Anakin's hometown of Mos Espa a larger version of Luke's native Mos Eisley. Mos Eisley's architecture was based on the building style of the Ibadite people of Djerba, an island off the coast of Tunisia. Ibadite structures are usually whitewashed and are characterized by a domed roof and few windows. For a little variety, ksar architecture was borrowed as well. Ksours (plural of ksar) were also built by the Berbers, and are multi-chambered fortress/granaries built of earth and stone.

The deserts of Tatooine became the location for the high-speed Podraces. As the film's race was being mapped out, and it was realized that vehicles travelling at several hundred miles per hour would cover vast expanses of terrain, Lucas requested that the art department create as many creatures as possible to dot the landscape. And so, led by concept artist/creature designer Terryl Whitlatch, the artists created entire ecologies and food chains, featuring the Tatooine equivalents of armadillos, jackrabbits, prairie dogs, and coyotes, to name a few.

Since Tatooine is where beings go when they don't want to be found, the denizens of Tatooine are a motley, forlorn mix. Everyone, however, must deal with the elements, and thus nearly everyone wears some combination of rugged, leathery attire to protect themselves from the sun. In creating this clothing, the artists drew upon Arab, Central Asian, and African cultures, as well the occasional American motorcycle gang.

With respect to Podracers, speeders, and droids, all have to be built to handle the three constants of life on Tatooine: lack of resources, relentless heat, and whipping sand. As we see in the construction of C-3PO, much of the technology on Tatooine looks as if it has been scavenged from mechanical debris, and it exhibits a cobbled together, weather-beaten, post-apocalyptic appearance.

Ultimately, Tatooine is a vast, desolate junkyard, and like any junkyard, it's full of surprises and the occasional discarded treasure. One such surprise turns out to be Anakin Skywalker, a slave who ultimately helps to free distant Naboo from the yoke of the Trade Federation.

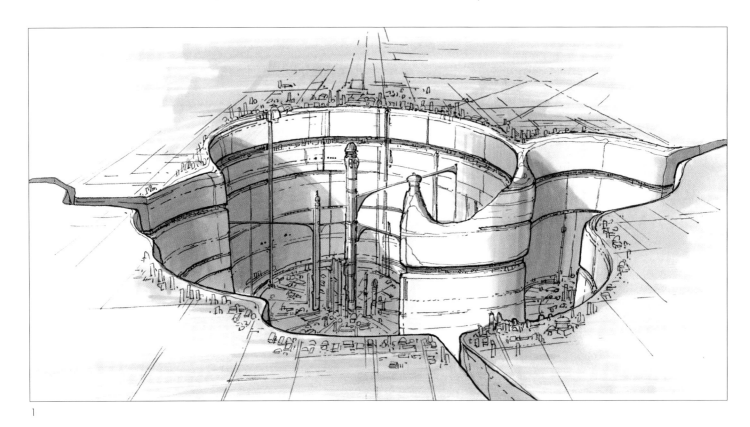

1

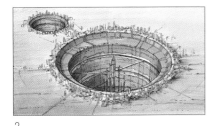

2

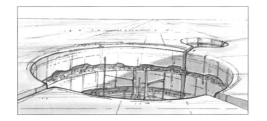

3

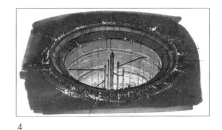

4

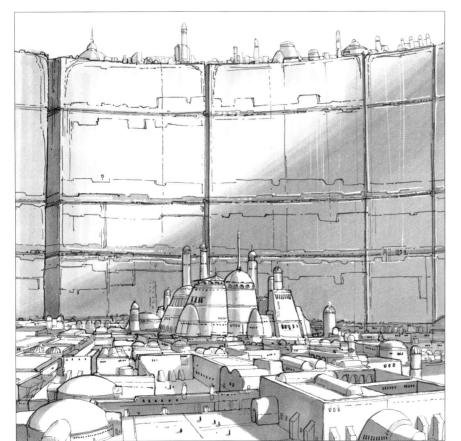

6

7

5

8

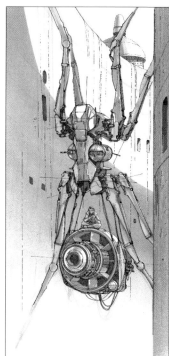

9

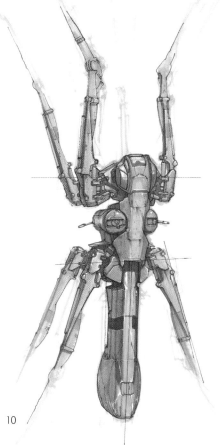

10

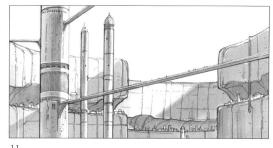

11

Mos Espa
1–11 Doug Chiang

Initially, Lucas and Chiang thought to take Luke Skywalker's pit house and expand it to city size for Mos Espa. The city would extend into the canyon walls, and cities would be connected to each other by manmade tunnel-canyons (1–8, 11).

Wall walker, conceptual designs (9. 10):
These spiderlike vehicles were to be used by smugglers to sneak illegal goods in and out of the pit cities.

Pages 128–129: Arena, architectural drawing for practical model
Bill Beck

1

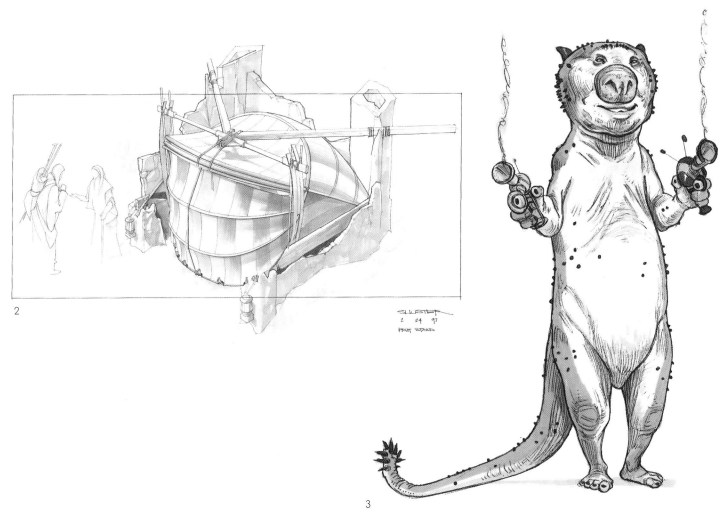

2

3

4

Mos Espa

1, 4, 5 Doug Chiang
2 Jay Shuster
3 Terryl Whitlatch

Jira's fruit stand and generic fruit stand, conceptual designs (1, 2)

Big-nosed alien, conceptual design:
Lucas saw a picture of a South American porcu-

pine and wanted to use a variation of it—with ray guns (3).

Mos Espa streets, conceptual designs:
Mos Espa was to be similar to Mos Eisley, but not *too* similar. Thus, while the architectural components are more or less the same, the skyline has a different character to it (4, 5). Hot-air balloons (4) were proposed as a popular means of transportation on Tatooine.

5

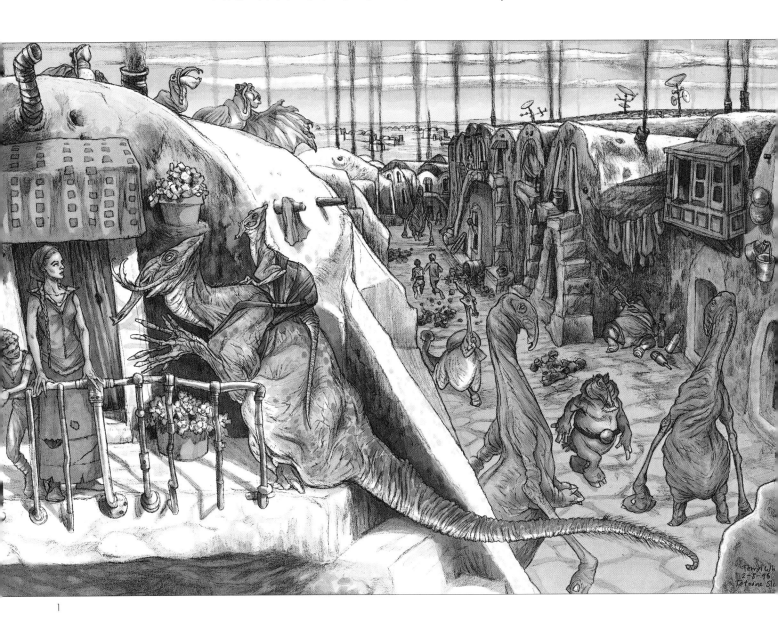

1

2

3

Mos Espa
1–6 Terryl Whitlatch

The crowded, bustling tenements (1, 2) where slaves such as Anakin Skywalker would live.

Thugs, conceptual designs:
This first bruiser is based on a rowdy member of the Hell's Angels (3), while the second one (6) can also be found in the *Star Wars: A New Hope: Special Edition* cantina scene.

Frog seller's booth, conceptual design (4)

Frog alien, conceptual design (5):
Although this fellow looks a bit like an early Gungan sketch, he was actually a separate creation, meant for the street vendors of Tatooine.

1

2

3

Podrace arena

1, 4, 5 *Doug Chiang*
2 *John Goodson*
3 *Brian Flora*
6 *Bill Beck*

Conceptual designs (1, 4)

Styrene and plaster conceptual model (2)

Matte painting (3)

Start/finish line, conceptual design (5) and architectural drawing for ILM production model (6)

4

5

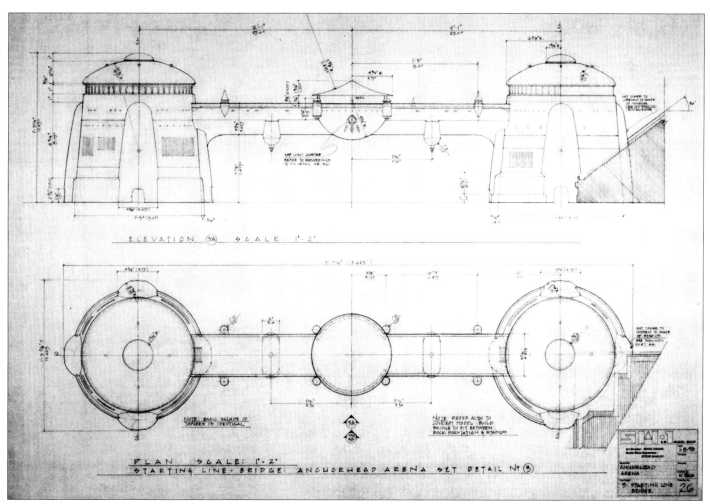

ELEVATION (3A) SCALE: 1'-2'

PLAN SCALE: 1'-2'
STARTING LINE BRIDGE: ANCHORHEAD ARENA SET DETAIL Nº (3)

6

1

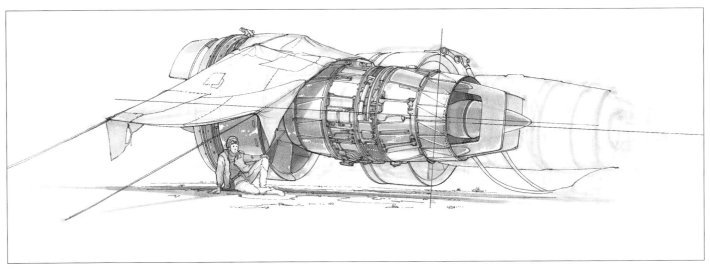

2

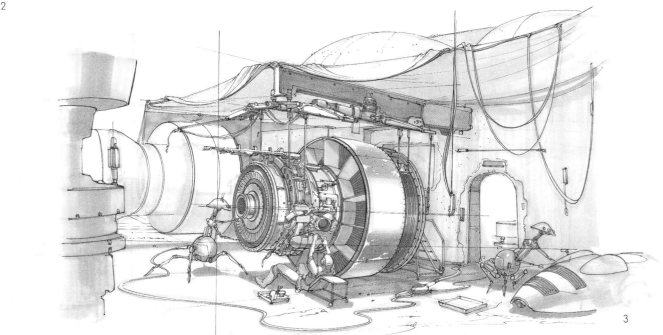

3

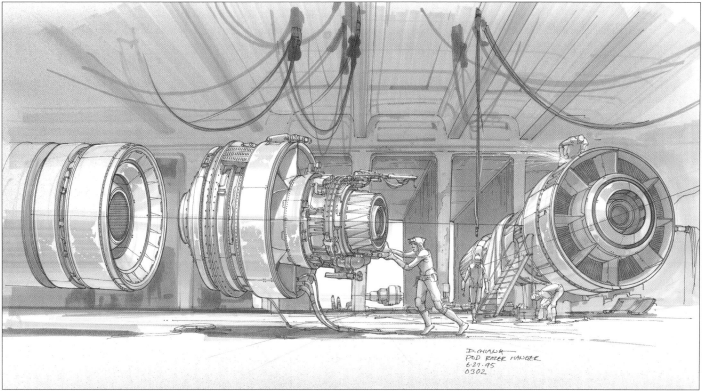

4

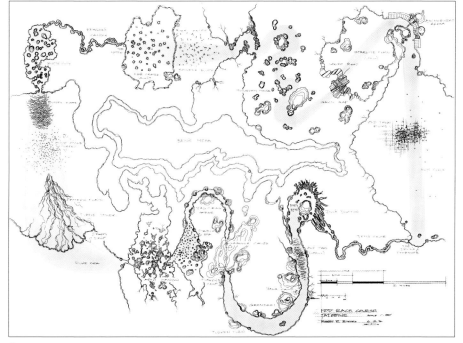

5

Podrace preparations

1–4, 6 Doug Chiang
5 Robert Barnes

Arena hangar, exterior, conceptual design (1): Chiang wanted to convey the sense of a horserace to the Podrace, and so he broke the hangar down into separate "stalls."

Podracer sitting in the shade waiting for the start of the race, conceptual design (2)

Anakin's backyard garage, conceptual design (3)

Arena hangar interior, conceptual design (4) and storyboard (6)

Podrace course, schematic map (5)

6

139

1

2

3

Podrace preparations
1, 2, 5 Doug Chiang
3, 4, 6–8 Terryl Whitlatch
7 Iain McCaig

Salvage dealers, conceptual designs (2):
Chiang wanted to inhabit Tatooine with as many oddities as possible, so he created "balloon wagons" for towing junk.

The Podraces also provide an opportunity for entrepreneurs to buy and sell. Salvage dealers haul their wares to the Podrace in the hopes of selling spare parts to racers and wannabes (1–3).

Fode/Beed Annodue, conceptual designs (4, 6–8)

Fode/Beed Annodue's announcer's booth, conceptual design (5)

4

5

6

7

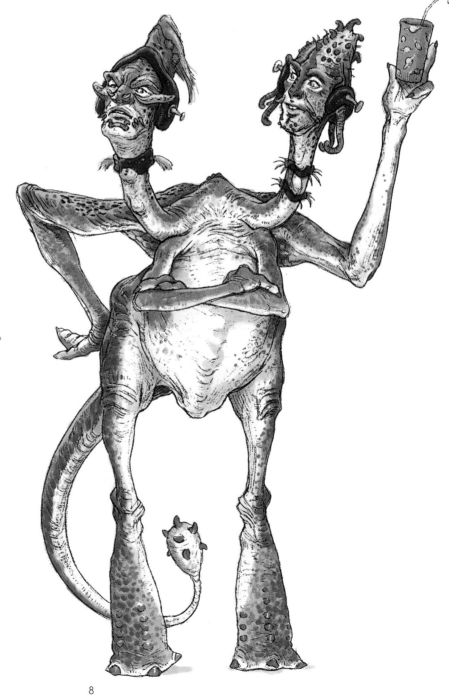

8

1

2

Podrace preparations

1, 4 Terryl Whitlatch
2 Jay Shuster
3 Iain McCaig
5 Kun Chang
6–11 Doug Chiang

Jabba the Hutt's box seats, conceptual designs
(1, 5)

Watto's box seats, conceptual design (2)

Jabba the Hutt, expression studies (3)

3   4

5

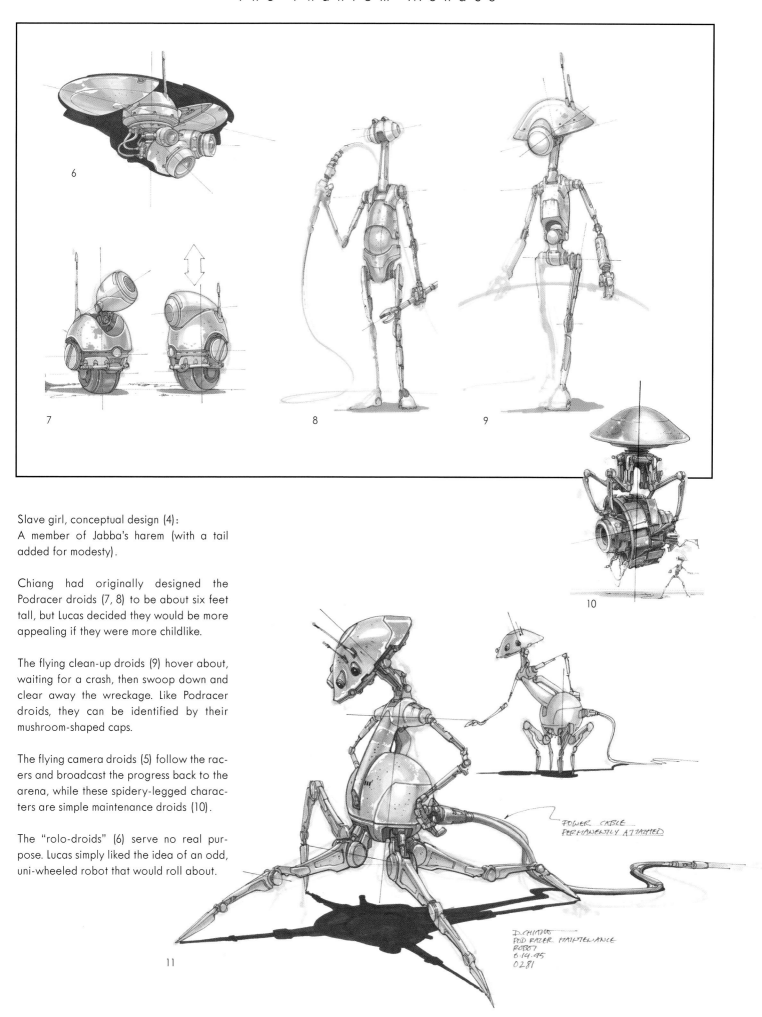

6

7

8

9

10

11

Slave girl, conceptual design (4):
A member of Jabba's harem (with a tail added for modesty).

Chiang had originally designed the Podracer droids (7, 8) to be about six feet tall, but Lucas decided they would be more appealing if they were more childlike.

The flying clean-up droids (9) hover about, waiting for a crash, then swoop down and clear away the wreckage. Like Podracer droids, they can be identified by their mushroom-shaped caps.

The flying camera droids (5) follow the racers and broadcast the progress back to the arena, while these spidery-legged characters are simple maintenance droids (10).

The "rolo-droids" (6) serve no real purpose. Lucas simply liked the idea of an odd, uni-wheeled robot that would roll about.

POWER CABLE
PERMANENTLY ATTACHED

D. CHIANG
POD RACER MAINTENANCE
ROBOT
6.14.95
0281

1

The Podrace
1–6 Doug Chiang

Racing through the arena, conceptual designs (1, 6)

Viewing platforms, conceptual designs: Originally the viewing platforms were capable of flight (2). However, when Lucas decided to use them in the Senate chamber instead, the Podrace viewing platforms were modified into elevator-type structures (5). Alternate proposals suggested by Chiang called for the viewing platforms to be suspended by hot-air balloons (3, 4).

2

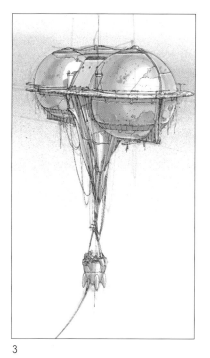

3

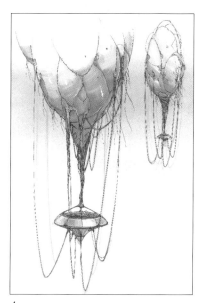

4

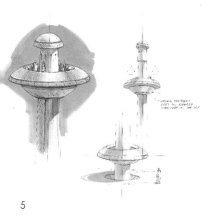

5

6

1

2

3

4

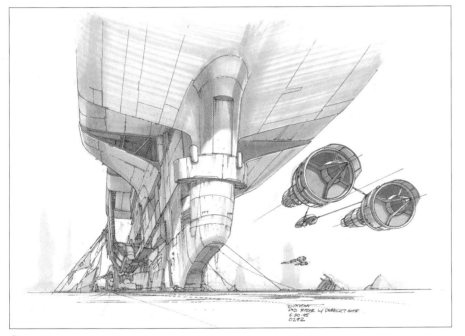

5

The Podrace course
1–6 Doug Chiang

Chiang created conceptual designs for a variety of obstacles and environments that would appear throughout the Podrace course. Among them were an arch canyon (1), a version of Beggar's Canyon that was inhabited by cliff dwellers (4), and a region littered by derelict ships (5). The last was cut because Lucas thought that the wrecks would be too confusing.

Digital conceptual paintings (2, 3, 6)

6

1

Anakin riding an eopie, towing salvage
1—3 Doug Chiang

In this early production painting (1) and conceptual design (2), Chiang depicted one of the
first versions of Anakin, the Podracers, and the
beast of burden that evolved into the kaadu
and the eopie. Once Lucas decided to turn the
two-legged eopie into the kaadu, Chiang
revised the eopie production painting by digitally grafting on two more legs (3).

2

3

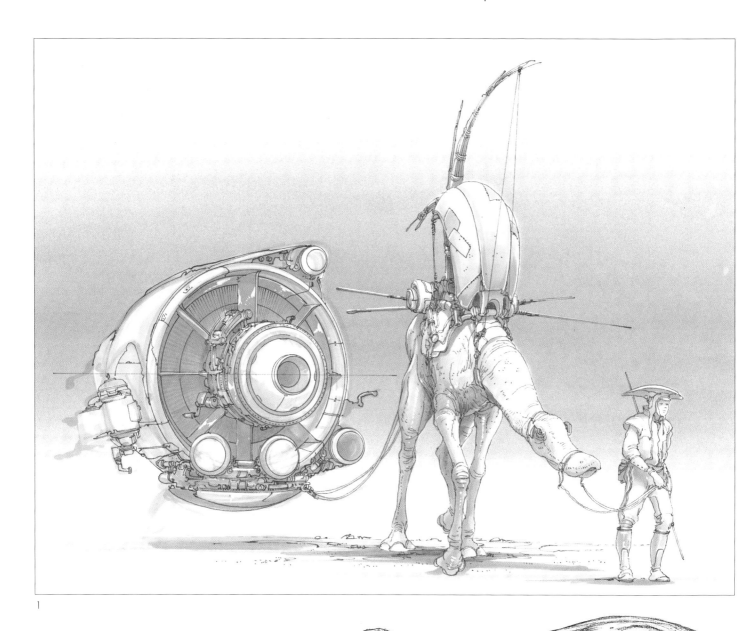

1

Animal life
1 Doug Chiang
2, 4–8 Terryl Whitlatch
3 Mark Siegel/Robert Barnes

Eopie towing salvage, revised four-legged conceptual design (1)

Eopie, conceptual design (2)

Anakin riding an eopie, Sculpey conceptual maquette (3)

A detailed ecology was constructed for Tatooine, though very little of it appears in the final film. Hungry coyotes/hyenas (5) wait for more Podrace casualties to munch on (they were replaced later by Tusken Raiders).

Given the harshness of life on Tatooine, the "prairie dogs and jackrabbits from hell" can't afford to be cute and fuzzy (7, 8), while other creatures, such as the "armadillos" (6) have developed tough, bony armor to protect them-

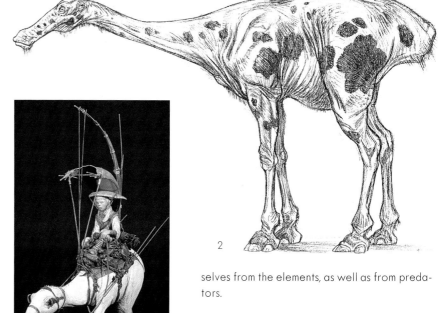

3

2

selves from the elements, as well as from predators.

Whitlatch sought to give her creations a visual focus, something that made each unique, without losing its sense of realism. In the case of the "vultures" (4), the focus was the bird's head, specifically the striking eye color.

4

5

6

7

8

1

2

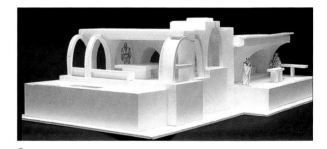

3

4

Anakin Skywalker

1, 2, 5, 6 Iain McCaig
3 Gavin Bocquet/production design team
4 Peter Walpole

Podrace helmets, initial and finished conceptual designs (1, 2)

Home in the slave quarters, conceptual card model (3)

Home, interior, finished set decoration (4)

Anakin's friend Wald, conceptual sketch (5)

Initial conceptual drawing (6)

5

1

C-3PO
1–4 Doug Chiang

Conceptual painting and designs:
Rather than have C-3PO be completely unstructured, the initial idea was to have him sport an automotive-type substructure (1). Lucas, however, felt that this was a little too structured, and Chiang "disassembled" the droid (2, 4) until Lucas was satisfied (3).

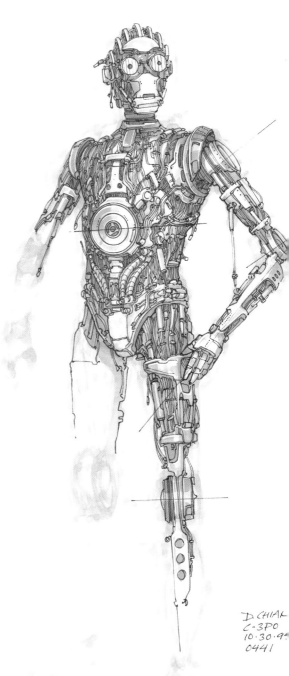

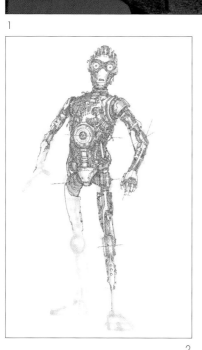

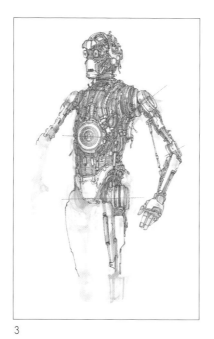

2   3   4

5

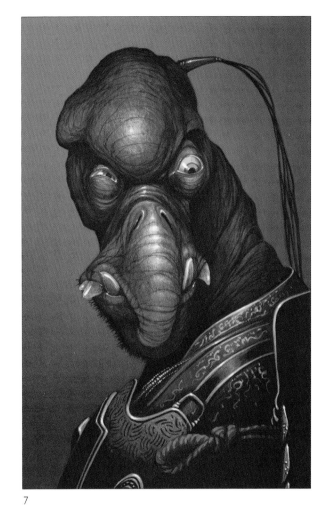

7

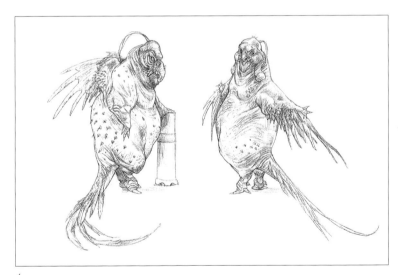

6

8

Watto

5, 7 Doug Chiang
6 Terryl Whitlatch
8 Iain McCaig

Watto, conceptual painting (7):
Initially, this was to be a portrait of a Neimoidian. Lucas had described the Neimoidians as pirate/mercenaries, so Chiang created this noble-looking, armor-wearing creature. Lucas was particularly taken with the face, however, and decided that it fit Watto's character better.

Final conceptual design (5)

Alternate versions of Watto, conceptual designs:
Before Lucas decided to turn the Neimoidian painting into Watto, Whitlatch and McCaig had created these "gobbley" (6) and "walrusy" (8) variants.

1

2

3

4

5

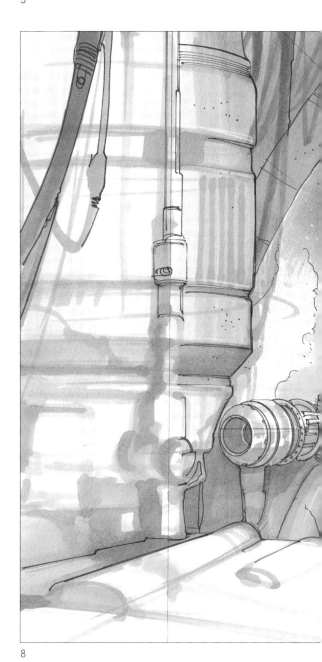

8

6

7

Watto
1–3 Iain McCaig
4 Robert Barnes
5, 6–8 Doug Chiang

Expression studies (1–3)

Conceptual maquette (4)

A digital painting (5) was used to define Watto's proportions, skin color, and wrinkle patterns.

Junk shop, conceptual designs:
At first, Watto's shop was based on standard Tatooine/Djerba-style architecture (7), but Lucas preferred a smokestack-like design (6). The interior was designed accordingly (8).

1

Sebulba
1, 2, 5 Terryl Whitlatch
3, 4, Iain McCaig
6 Iain McCaig (based on work by Jay Shuster)

Expression studies (1, 3, 4)

Sebulba and Anakin, early conceptual design (2)

Color and skeletal orthographics:
Lucas liked the idea of a "spidery character" that walked on his hands and drove with his feet, but he had to be small and light for the pod. The idea for Sebulba's face (3, 4) came from a camel with a bad attitude, while his color scheme came from an Easter egg (1, 5, 6). The tusks were ultimately dropped to make it easier for the digital artists to lip-sync him. Sebulba, like every other creature in the film, had a skeleton (5) created to provide detailed anatomical reference for the animators.

Sebulba's racing outfit (6) was heavily influenced by medieval armor. Lucas wanted his goggles to be huge, with magnifying lenses that would distort and enlarge his eyes, to make him even scarier.

2

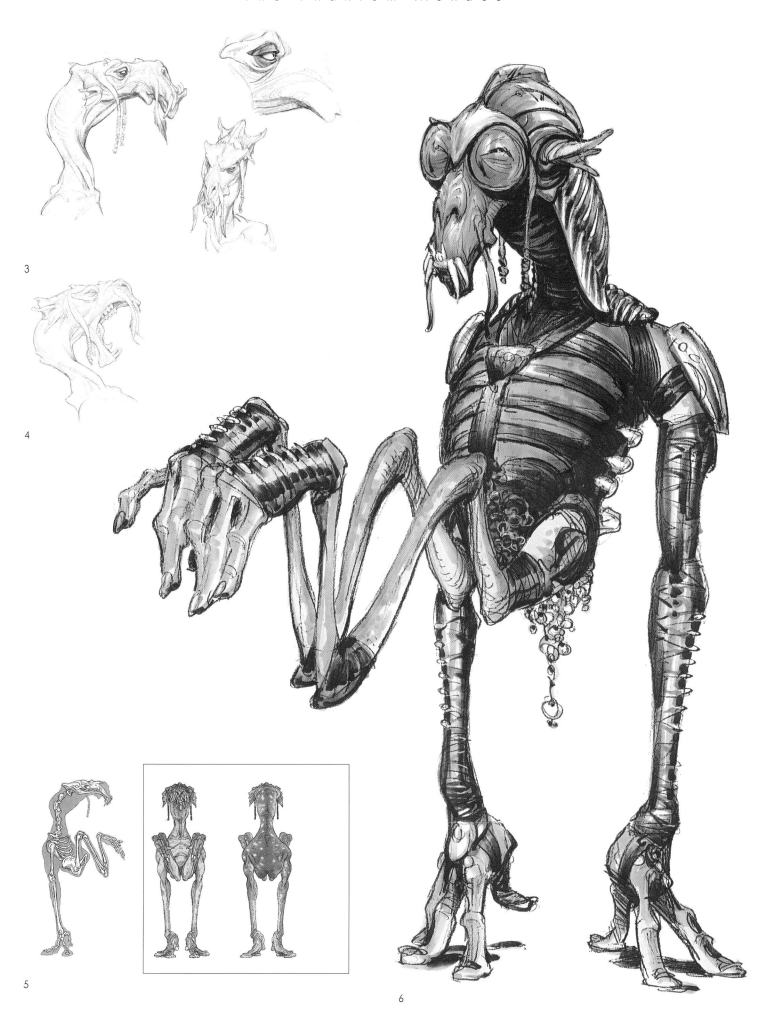

3

4

5

6

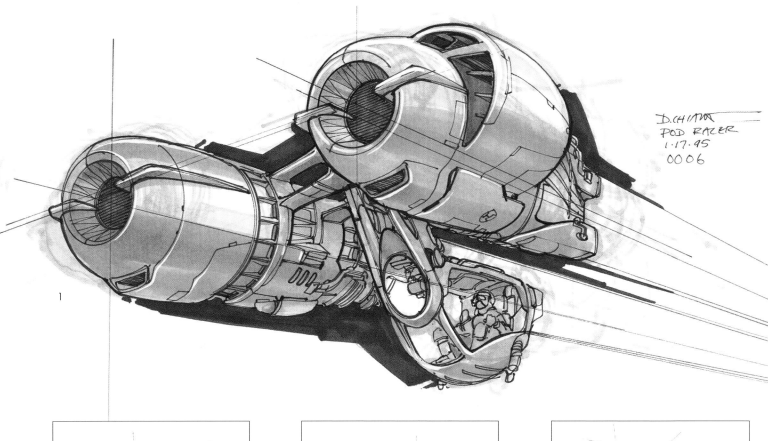

D.CHIANG
POD RACER
1·17·95
0006

1

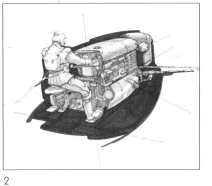

2

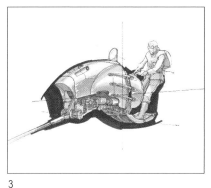

3

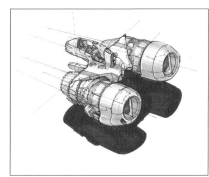

4

Podracers

1–11 Doug Chiang

The early conceptual designs for the cockpits were created at the same time that Chiang was designing the STAPs, hence the near-standing positions for the pilots. This first design (2) was based on a tractor. The pilot would sit on a tiny seat and wear a seat-belt-type harness. Another sketch (3) was influenced by a powered water ski. Both versions were dropped because Lucas wanted more protective cockpits.

Lucas had only described the Podracers as "two jet engines and a cockpit." This led to Chiang's earliest interpretations (1, 4, 5), after which Lucas decided the engines should be loosely tethered to the cockpit. While the subsequent design (6) appeared too rigid, it was the first step in the right direction.

Aldar Beedo's and Gasgano's Podracers, conceptual designs (7, 10)

Sebulba's Podracer, early conceptual designs (8, 9, 11)

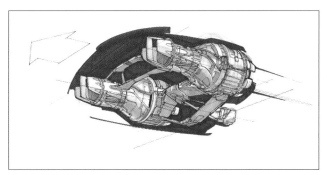

5

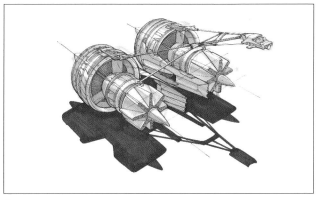

6

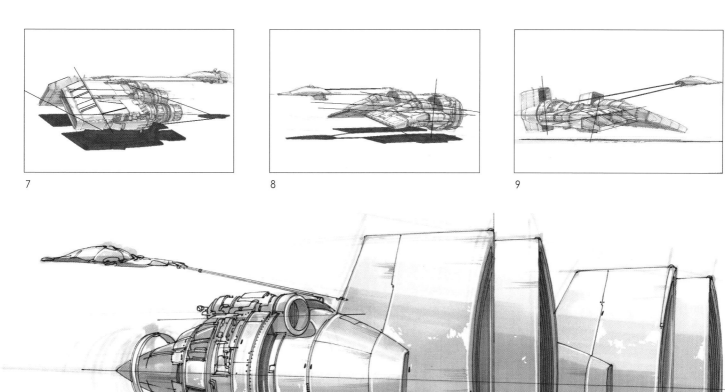

7

8

9

10

D. CHIALUS
POD RACER
10.19.95
0422

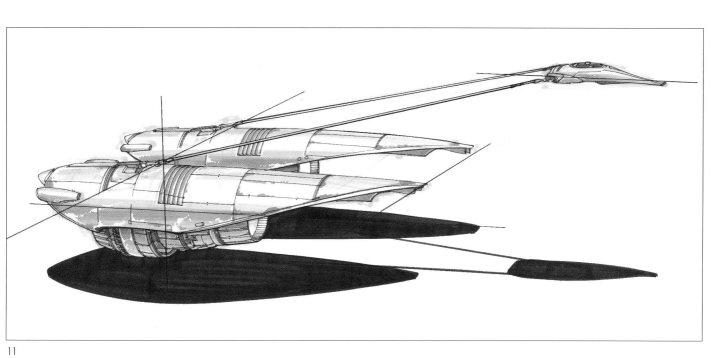

11

1

Podracers
1, 3 Doug Chiang
2 John Goodson

This digitally-altered production painting of the Podrace (1) was originally cropped in to just above the engines. Lucas saw it and decided that the cockpit should be included in the frame. Chiang used a computer to revise the painting accordingly and to

add motion blur—something that would have been very hard to do without the benefit of digital technology.

Early styrene, brass, and wood conceptual model (2): This cockpit, originally intended for Anakin, became Gasgano's, while the engines went to Ratts Tyerell.

Anakin's Podracer, digital production painting (3).

2

3

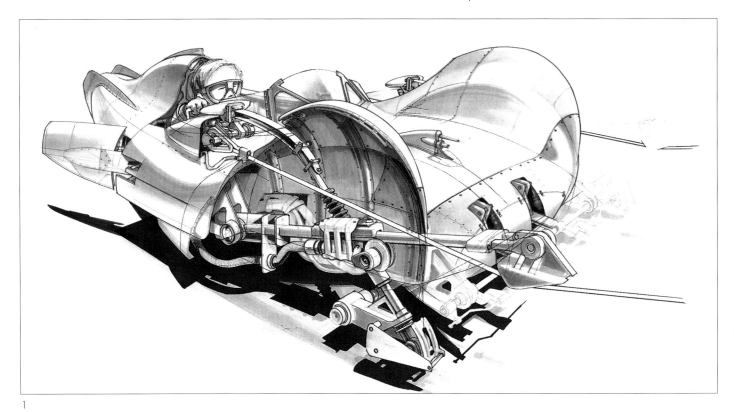

1

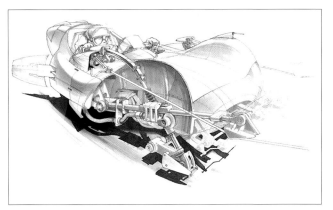

2

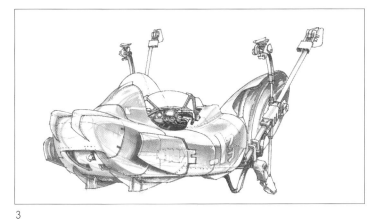

3

Anakin and his Podracer

1–3, 5, 6, 8, 9 Jay Shuster
4 Doug Chiang
7 Iain McCaig

Anakin Skywalker, conceptual design (7)

Podracer conceptual design (1–4, 6, 8, 9)

Podracer conceptual model (5)

Jay Shuster: "George is a big race car fan, so in my mind I created the perfect, imaginary race car, then modified it for Anakin's cockpit (1). Its front fenders became air foils and control arm shields which would nicely frame Anakin in a shot. I added the hyper-mechanical elements, and the sloped headrest, and finished the back end with airbrakes and a classic ducktail. A larger, clearer windshield was later added so as not to obscure Anakin when shot from the front, and a few modifications were made to the tail and hood, as well." (2, 5)

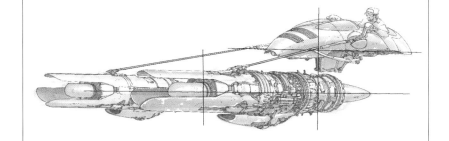

4

5

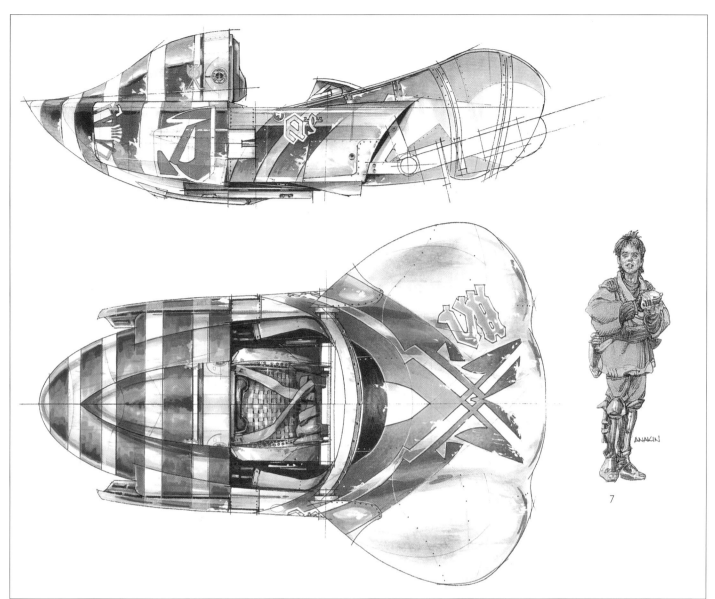

7

6

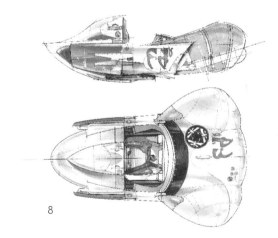

8

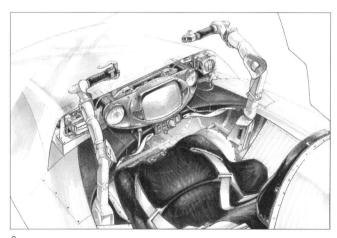

9

Originally, Anakin's cockpit was to have large, mechanical control arms (3) that would articulate into place from an "up" position. Lucas had wanted tall control arms so that Anakin's steering actions would be accentuated. This design, unfortunately, worked better on paper than in reality. The large screen (9) in the center of the dashboard is the rearward video viewer and race status–tracking monitor.

In one early scheme (8), the Japanese moth motif (the black circle on the lower drawing) showed the pilot's youth. Ultimately, a striped design (6) from a sports car Lucas owned in his youth was used so that Anakin's Podracer would stand out from the rest. Other symbols included a "Hutt sanctioning body" logo, pseudo–Native American wing motifs on the air-brake tips, and a Skywalker emblem on the sloping headrest. The red character on the air brake is both a numeral and a lower case "a," identifying Anakin's cockpit.

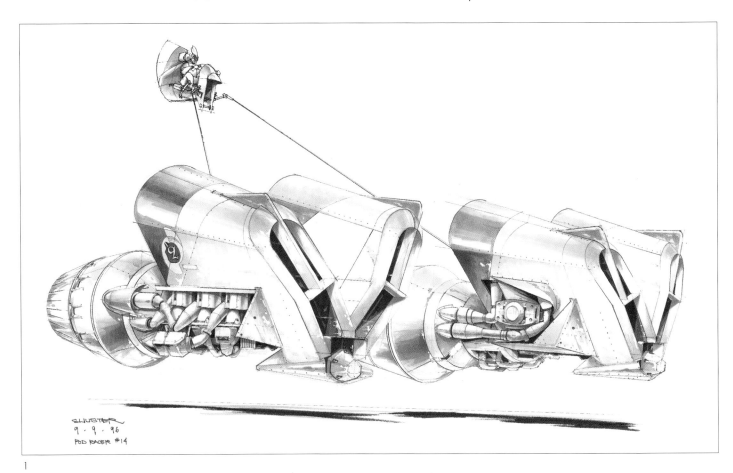

1

Sebulba's Podracer
1–2 Jay Shuster

Intermediate conceptual design:
Inspired by the classic V8 engine (1), these Podracer engines were placed at ninety degree angles in order to create an "X"-shaped look.

According to Jay Shuster, the final conceptual design (2) "is based on a fighter jet. The tail of the Podracer is the nose of the jet and the exhaust pipe in the back was originally a gattling gun. The headrest is the jet pilot's heads-up screen and control panel, and the cylindrical drums to either side are the plane's engines. Sebulba's has them arranged as the primary control arm pylons, each containing an array of hydraulic and compression clutch-drive systems that control the cables that drive his engines. As for the colors, well, I really love orange. Paired with black and white, the Podracer's contrasting values make it one of the most electric color schemes in the field. This color grouping is based on my dad's car's paint job. The graphic on the Podracer also borrows from his car, as well as the Swiss flag's white cross. Finally, the texture on the control-arm cylinders is derived from Islamic art, and the engine graphics are rave-influenced."

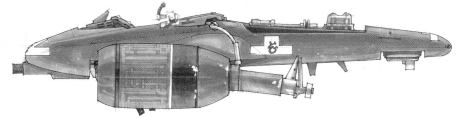

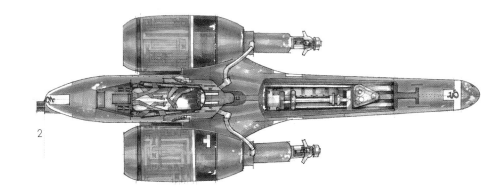

2

Podracer graphics, conceptual designs
3, 4 Jay Shuster
5, 6 Jay Shuster (based on Podracer designs by Gavin Bocquet/production

Jay Shuster: "Aldar Beedo's cockpit (3) is based on the model race cars my brother built when he was a kid. I began by sketching a generic show-car, and replaced the tires with spoilers. I then turned the body over and around. It has an above average number of air brakes/control surfaces/spoilers, a graphic scheme sporting a sunburst, phoenixlike motif, and smaller emblems drawn from fifteenth-century England."

Anakin Skywalker's cockpit and engines, top and side view (4)

Mawhonic's cockpit (5)

Teemto Pagalies' cockpit (6)

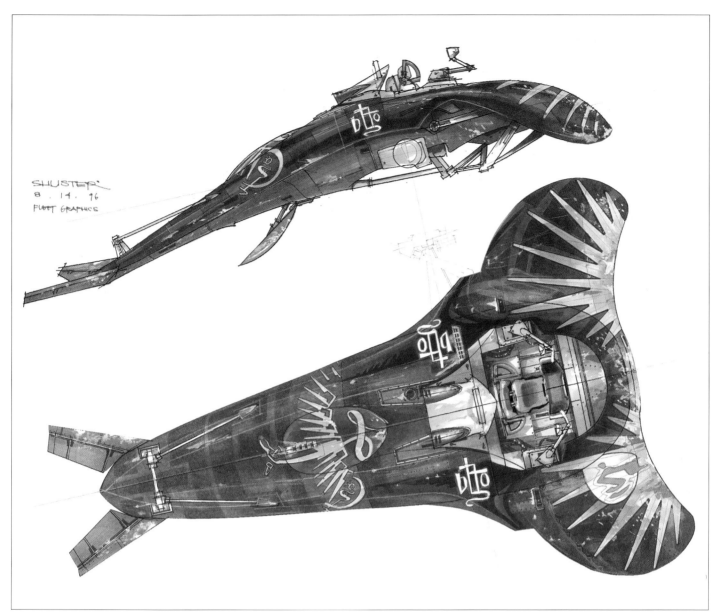

SHUSTER
8 . 14 . 96
FLEET GRAPHICS

3

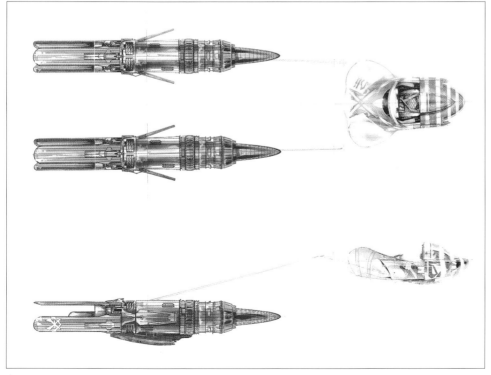

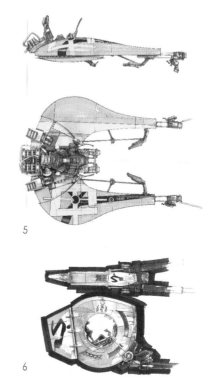

4

5

6

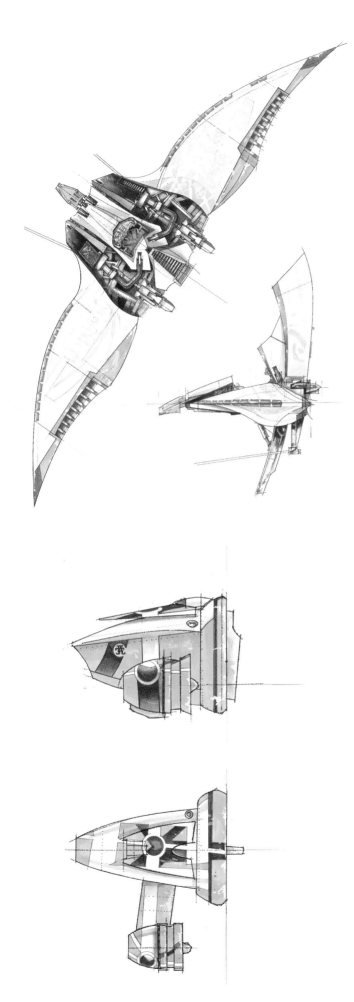

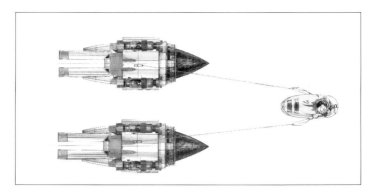

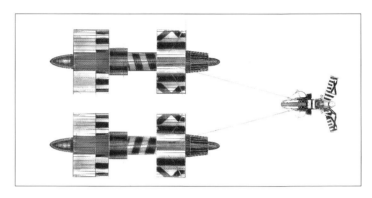

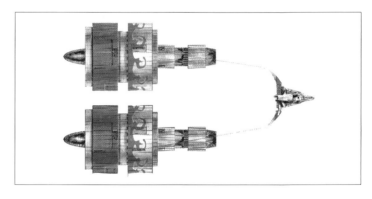

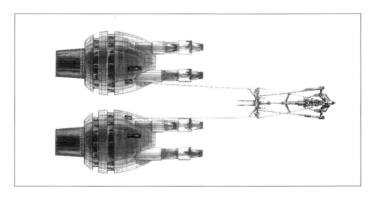

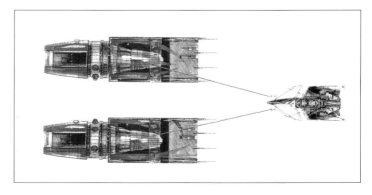

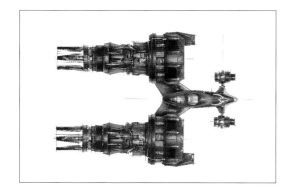

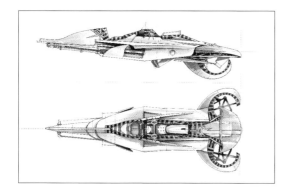

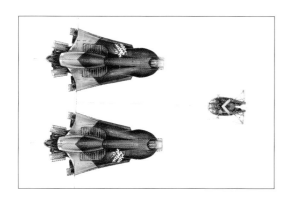

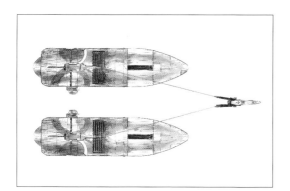

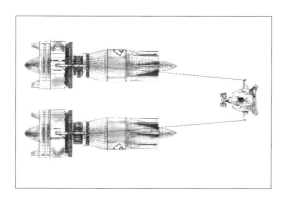

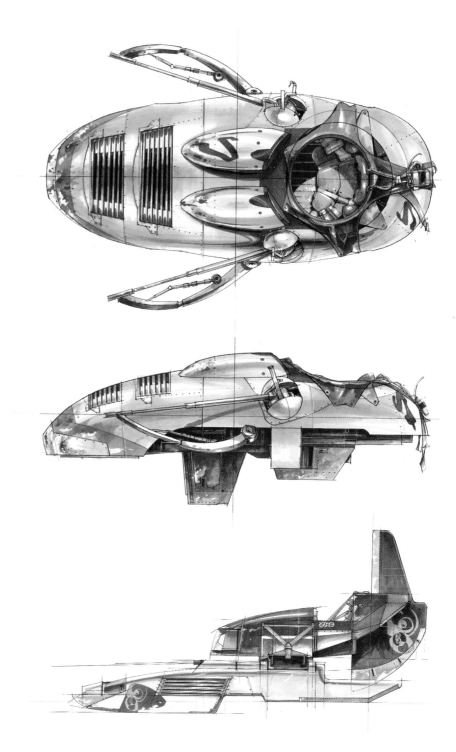

Podracer graphic schemes
Jay Shuster (applied to Podracers created by the concept and production design teams)

Each graphic scheme was designed so that each Podracer might be picked out of the crowd. This was critical because each Podracer would have relatively little screen time, and would be moving very quickly, making them difficult to distinguish.

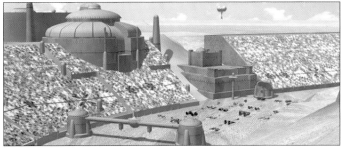

1

2

3

4

5

6

7

8

9

10

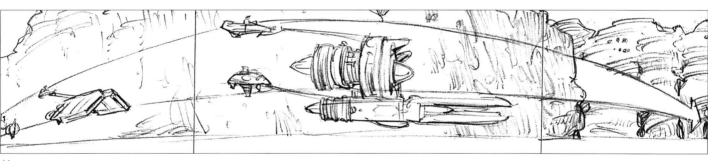

11

12

13

Podrace—first lap, selected storyboards and animatic frames
1, 3, 5, 9 David Dozoretz
2, 4, 6–8, 11–13 Iain McCaig
10 Edwin Natividad

Every shot of the Podrace was meticulously mapped out, first as hundreds of storyboards, then later as rigorously executed computer animatics. The art department worked closely with editors Ben Burtt and Martin Smith to provide Lucas with a precise cut of the Podrace which could be used to show ILM and the production crew exactly what was required.

Podracer pilots, conceptual designs
1–5, 7 Terryl Whitlatch
6 Richard Mills/Robert Barnes

Dud Bolt (1)
Neva Kee (2)
Mawhonic (3)
Aldar Beedo (4)
Teemto Pagalies (5)
Gasgano, conceptual maquette (6)
Ebe Endocott (7)

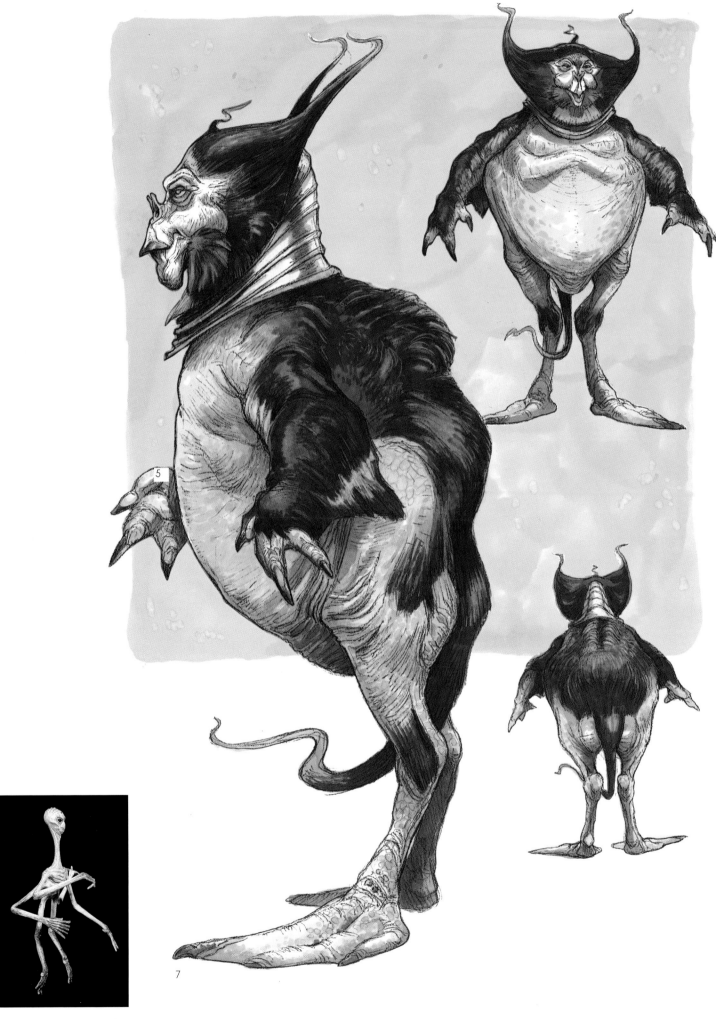

5

6

7

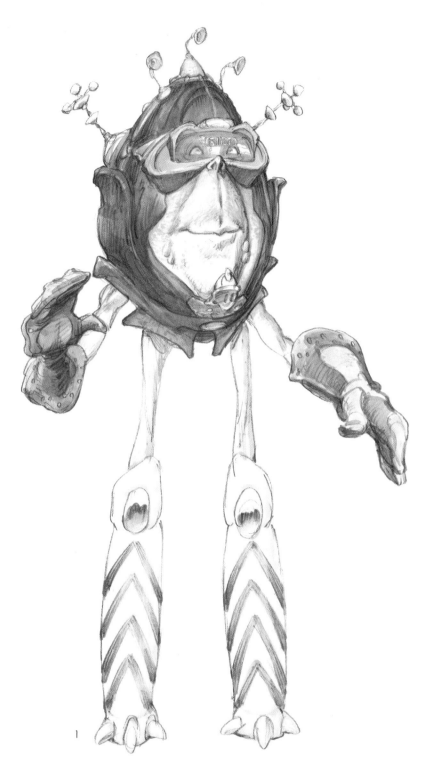

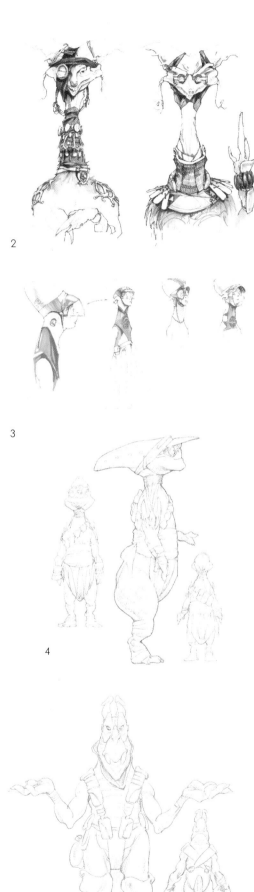

Podracer pilots, conceptual designs
1, 4 Iain McCaig
2, 3 Jay Shuster
5, 6–10 Terryl Whitlatch

Ben Quadinaros, with costume (1)
Bozzie Baranta, with costume (2)
Ody Mandrell (3)
Ratts Tyerell, with costume (4), without costume (7)
Teemto Pagalies, with costume (5)
Boles Roar (6)
Mars Guo (8)
Ark "Bumpy" Roose (9)
Bullseye Navior (10)

6

7

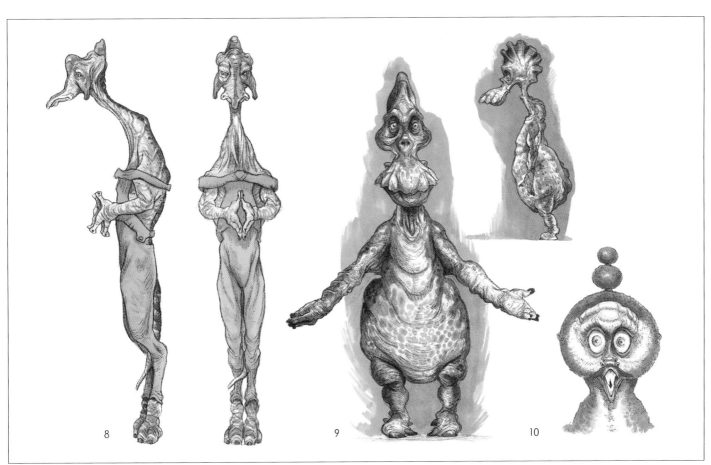

8

9

10

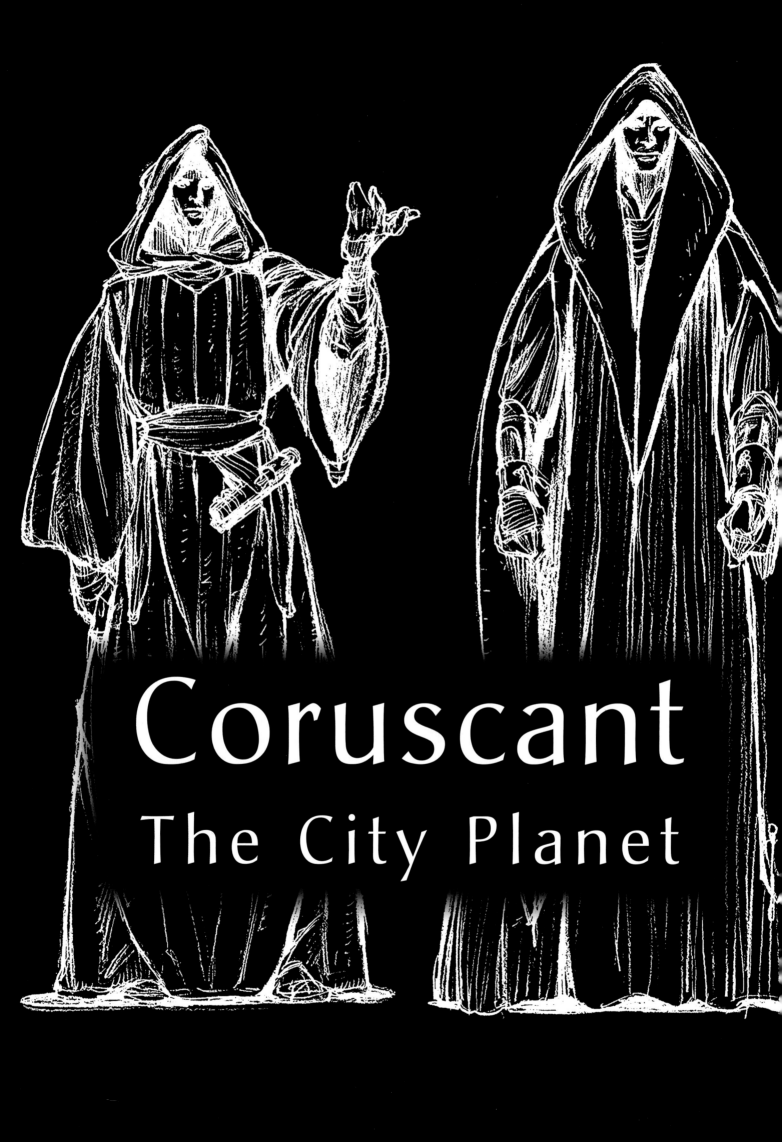

Coruscant
The City Planet

Notable for its polish and grace, the elegant geometry of the art deco style is identified with affluence and power. Hence, it proved to be the perfect style for Coruscant, the sparkling, cosmopolitan capital of the Republic.

A lot of the initial work on Coruscant had been done by Ralph McQuarrie in preparation for *Return of the Jedi*, but none of it was seen until the Special Edition release of that film. For *The Phantom Menace*, the art department had the opportunity to make use of McQuarrie's work and to take it even further. George Lucas had always described Coruscant as a planet covered by buildings—megastructures of glass, concrete, and steel, hundreds of times taller than what we see here on Earth. The city climbs so high that one must navigate it via flying taxis, which dock at rooftops and floating platforms, *à la The Empire Strikes Back's* Cloud City.

Depending on which region or "neighborhood" was being created, Coruscant's buildings were modeled either on the concrete look of New York's Empire State Building, or the metallic look of the Chrysler Building. The Empire State Building is famed for its multi-leveled edifice employing an architectural design known as "setbacks," suggestive of the staggering Central American and Egyptian pyramids. Since it has a columnar support originally built for the anchoring of dirigibles, it is also a particularly good model for designing buildings that could serve as docks for flying taxis. Fittingly enough, Senator Palpatine lives in an older neighborhood that has an appropriately "Empire State" look to it.

The Galactic Senate is the sun around which the Republic revolves. Thus, the buildings in the Senate's vicinity are capped by gleaming domes, and they sport bright, streamlined curves. The Senate itself is a massive dome in the heart of this "Chrysler Building" district, where representatives of countless worlds gather.

The one exception to Coruscant's predominant art deco style is the Jedi Temple. Lucas wanted the place where the Jedi convene to have a sense of sacredness to it, as well as a daunting dose of grandeur. As a result, the Jedi complex is a bit Gothic, a bit pyramidal, and a bit Chinese Forbidden City.

Given that Coruscant is the seat of government, its residents provide a wildly diverse mix of sentient beings, with little in common with one another beyond the fact that they are all there to conduct very important business. Although everyone is seen wearing their finest clothes, fashions vary radically from species to species. The only uniform to be found is that of the Senatorial guard, with their blue, Greco-Roman inspired plumes. So when it came time for the artists to create Coruscant's populace, they were afforded a great degree of freedom.

Coruscant's air taxis sport a fishlike shape, and Coruscant's airways are teeming with them, giving the sky the appearance of a sea filled with schools of exotic creatures. The floating feeling one gets as one travels about the city is there by design—Coruscant was crafted as a metaphor for the drifting nature of the Republic. One never sees the ground on Coruscant. It is a planet of comings and goings, where no one is firmly rooted. The Galactic Senate is similarly out of touch with the rest of the galaxy, and Naboo pays the price.

1

Coruscant cityscapes, conceptual designs and digital conceptual paintings
1–7 Doug Chiang

In Palpatine's "neighborhood" (1, 7), concrete structures hundreds of times the size of the Empire State Building predominate. More recently built sections, however, are sleeker, and built from glass and metal. Chiang based the shapes of these newer buildings (3) on cactus formations. Other districts boast architectural styles that combine the old and the new (6). No matter what the locale, though, the towers of Coruscant dwarf their occupants (5).

Digital paintings allowed the artists to duplicate elements and change their scale with greater ease. Chiang, for example, built an impressive skyline (2) in a relatively short period of time. Another painting meanwhile, originally a daytime shot of Palpatine's neighborhood, was digitally altered to create a sunset (4).

Pages 176–177: Obi-Wan Kenobi, conceptual designs
Iain McCaig

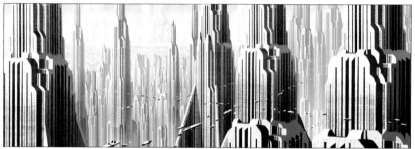

2

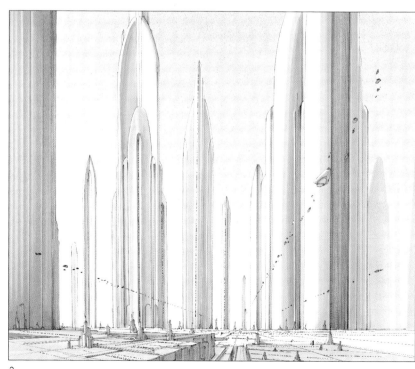

3

4

5

6

7

1

Coruscant cityscapes: the Galactic Senate's
neighborhood, digital conceptual paintings
1, 2 Doug Chiang

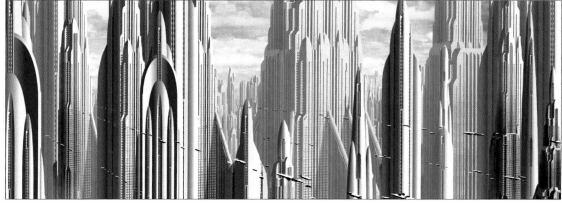

2

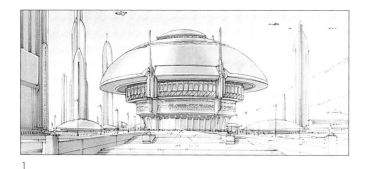

1

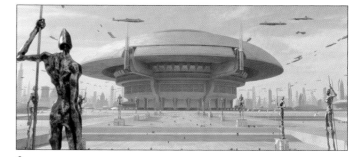

2

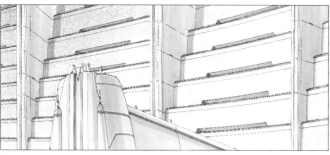

3

Galactic Senate

1, 3, 5–7, 9 Doug Chiang
2 Mark Sullivan
4 Edwin Natividad
8 Ryan Tudhope and Kevin Baillie

Storyboard and matte painting (1, 2)

Statue, conceptual design (4)

Originally, the senators were to sit in gigantic, terraced balconies, which would be connected to Chancellor Valorum's podium by a large walkway (3). However, once the floating platform design (9) was introduced, the layout of the chamber was redesigned. Each delegation was given its own floating platform and designated dock in the wall of the giant, bowl-shaped room (6). Standing in the very center of the chamber is the Chancellor's podium. (5).

Camera droid, conceptual design (7):
Originally designed to broadcast the Podrace, this droid was modified to record the proceedings of the Galactic Senate.

Senate chamber, animatic frame (8)

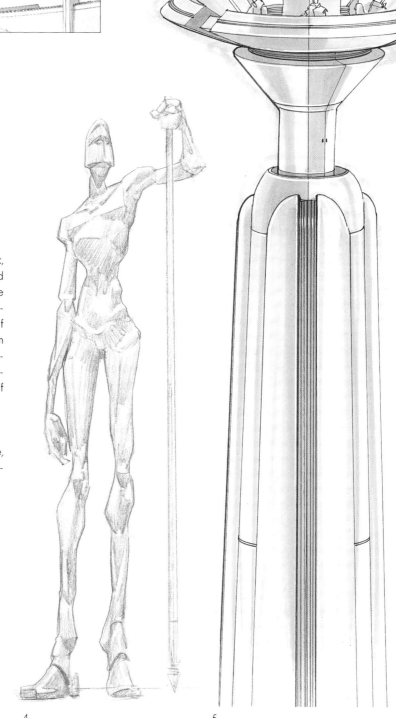

4

5

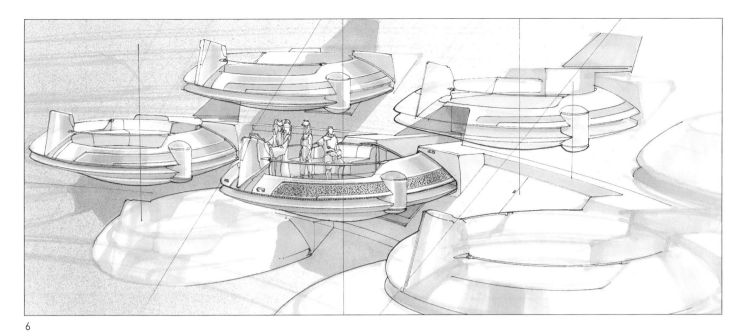

6

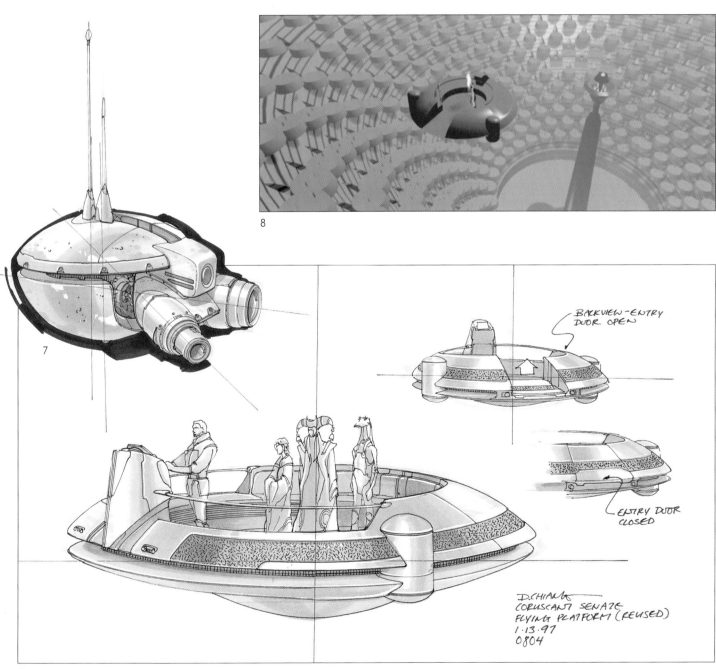

8

7

9

BACKVIEW-ENTRY
DOOR OPEN

ENTRY DOOR
CLOSED

D.CHIANG
CORUSCANT SENATE
FLYING PLATFORM (REUSED)
1·13·97
0804

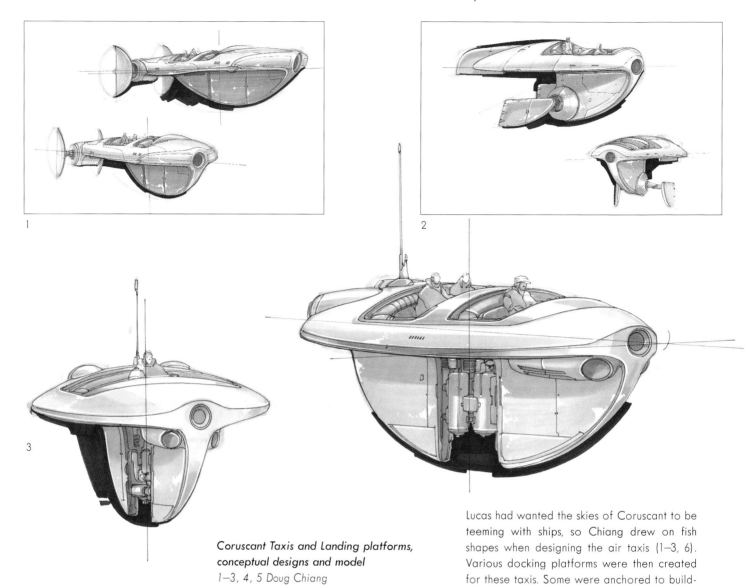

1

2

3

***Coruscant Taxis and Landing platforms,
conceptual designs and model***
1–3, 4, 5 Doug Chiang
6 John Goodson

Lucas had wanted the skies of Coruscant to be teeming with ships, so Chiang drew on fish shapes when designing the air taxis (1–3, 6). Various docking platforms were then created for these taxis. Some were anchored to buildings (4), whereas others would become part of the hovering landing platforms used by spaceships, such as Queen Amidala's (5).

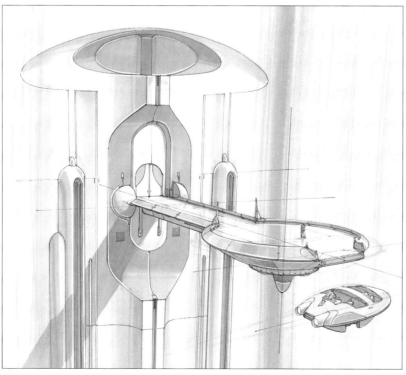

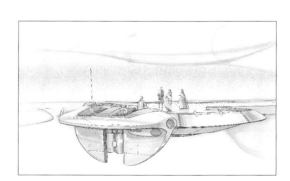

5

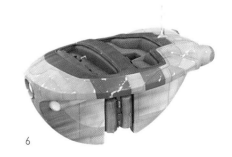

6

4

7

8

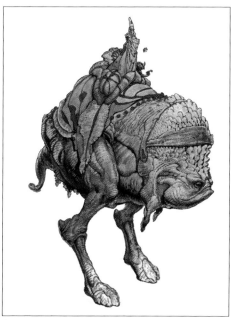

9

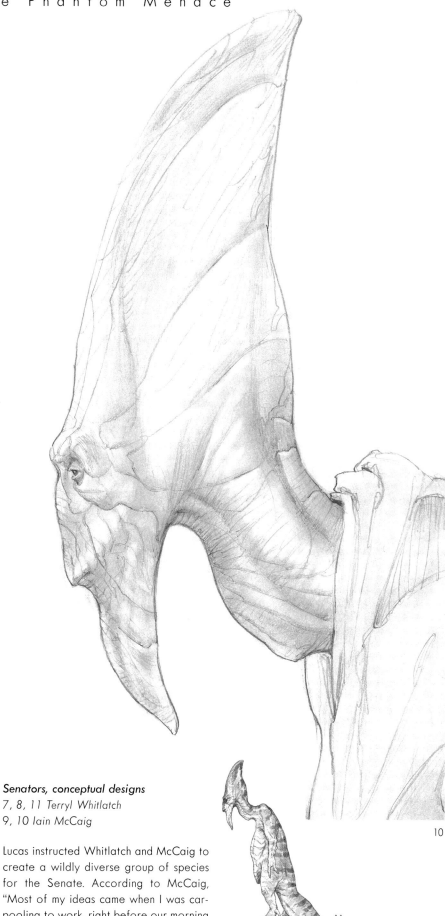

10

11

Senators, conceptual designs
7, 8, 11 Terryl Whitlatch
9, 10 Iain McCaig

Lucas instructed Whitlatch and McCaig to create a wildly diverse group of species for the Senate. According to McCaig, "Most of my ideas came when I was car-pooling to work, right before our morning meetings. So, I drew Senator Horox Ryyder (10) while bouncing along in the passenger seat, taking the occasional break to get over the nausea of motion sickness. Terryl [Whitlatch] later drew his body" (11).

Senator Mot-Not Rab (8), though, was not the product of car-induced nausea, but is, in fact, named after animatronic model designer/workshop supervisor Chris Barton's son, Tom.

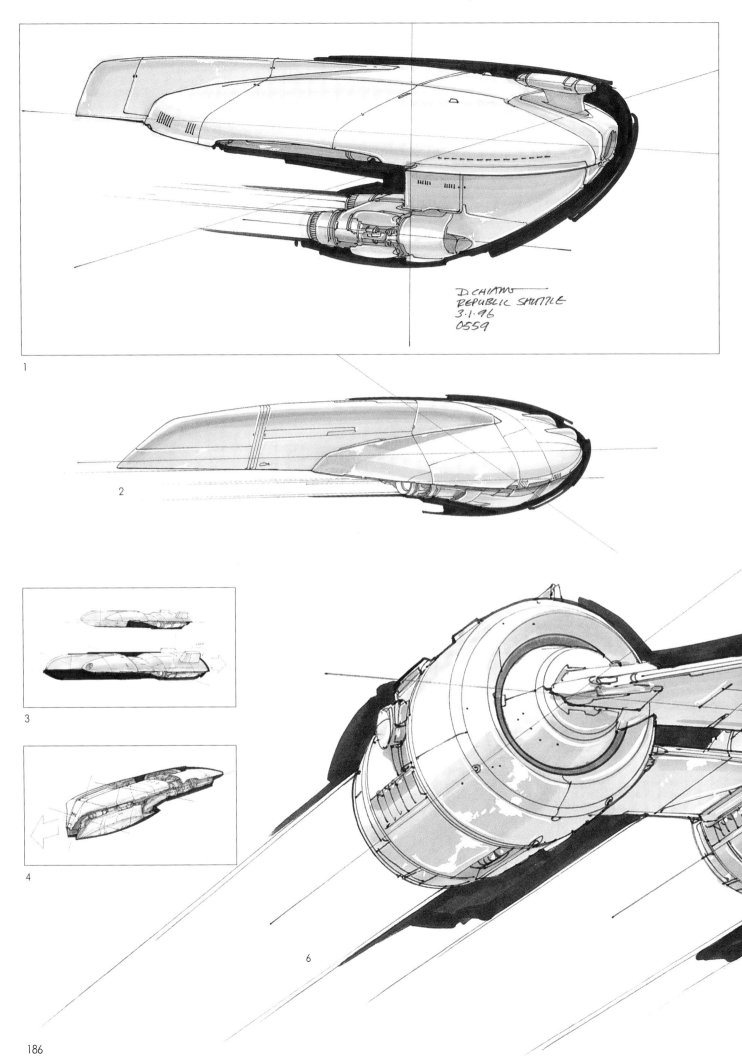

1

D CHIANG
REPUBLIC SHUTTLE
3.1.96
0559

2

3

4

6

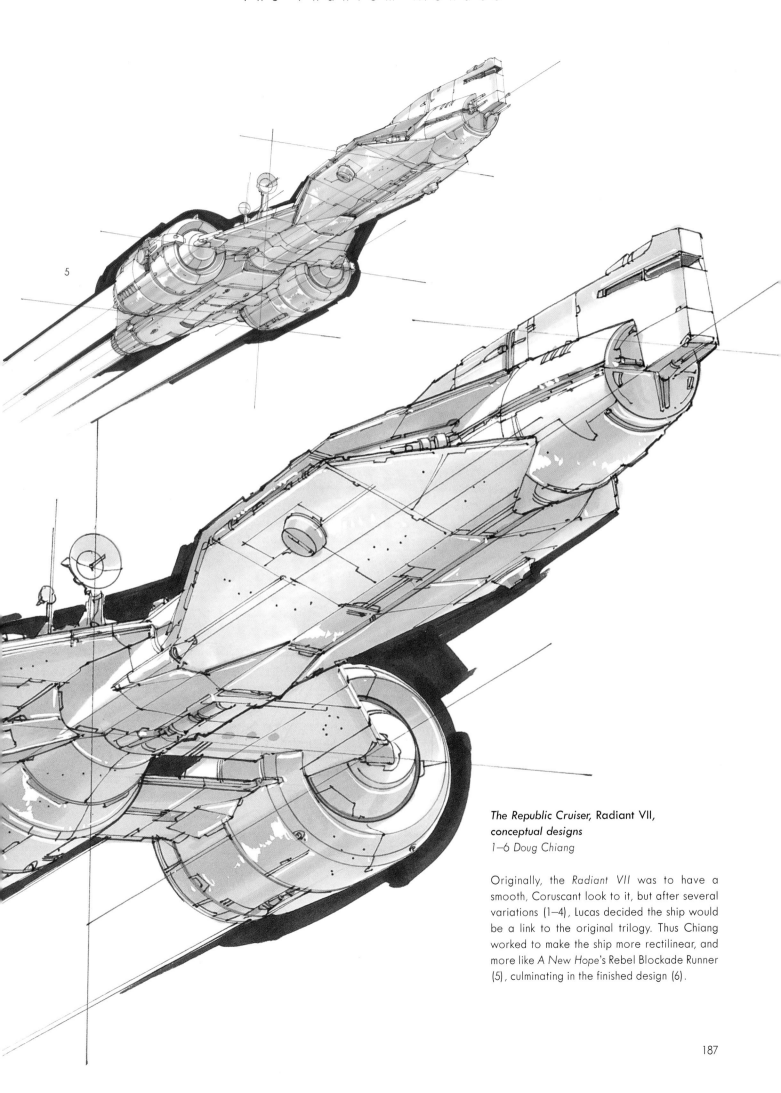

5

**The Republic Cruiser, Radiant VII,
conceptual designs**
1–6 Doug Chiang

Originally, the *Radiant VII* was to have a
smooth, Coruscant look to it, but after several
variations (1–4), Lucas decided the ship would
be a link to the original trilogy. Thus Chiang
worked to make the ship more rectilinear, and
more like *A New Hope*'s Rebel Blockade Runner
(5), culminating in the finished design (6).

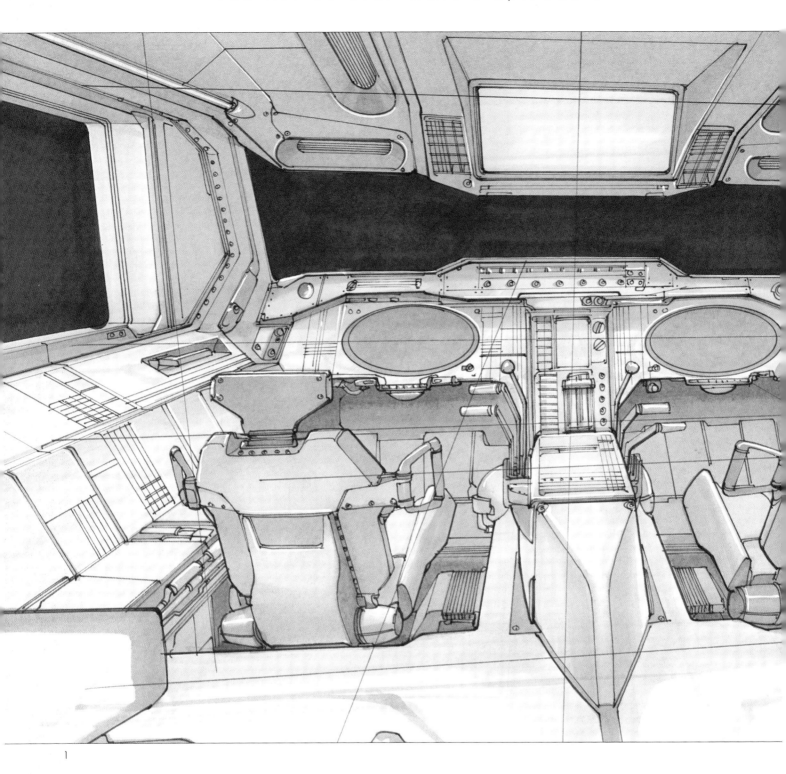

1

The Republic Cruiser, Radiant VII
1–3 Doug Chiang
4 John Goodson, ILM

Cockpit interior, conceptual design (1)

As John Goodson and ILM began to build the
Radiant VII production model (4), Lucas decided
that the ship needed "a little extra something"
added to the front to guide one's eyes to the
cockpit, so Chiang added little antennae and
wings (2, 3).

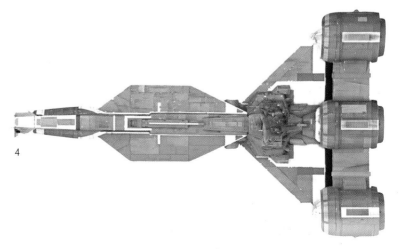

4

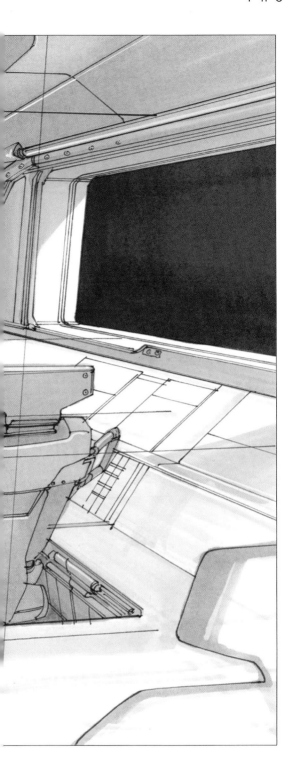

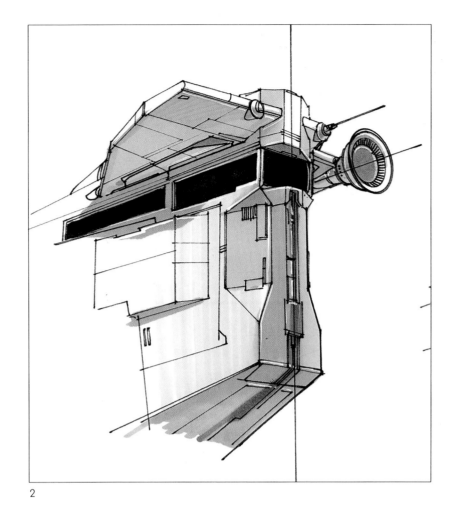

2

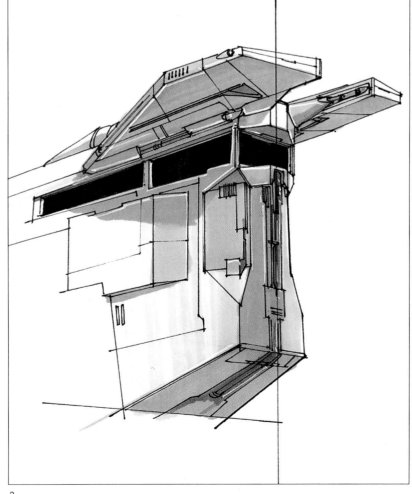

3

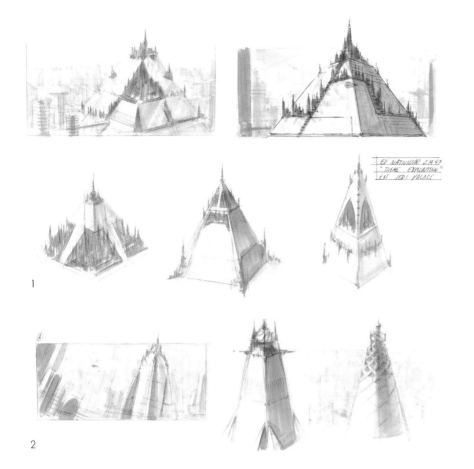

1

2

Jedi Temple and Plaza

1–6 Edwin Natividad
7 Kurt Kaufman

Conceptual designs (1-5):
The symbol of good in the galaxy, the sacred Jedi Temple is a hybrid of Gothic, art deco, and ancient Chinese and Egyptian architecture.

Storyboard (6)

Plan view (7)

3

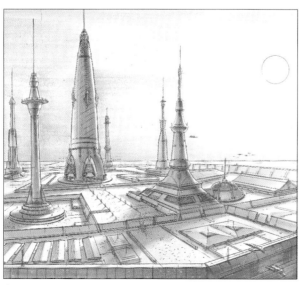

4

5

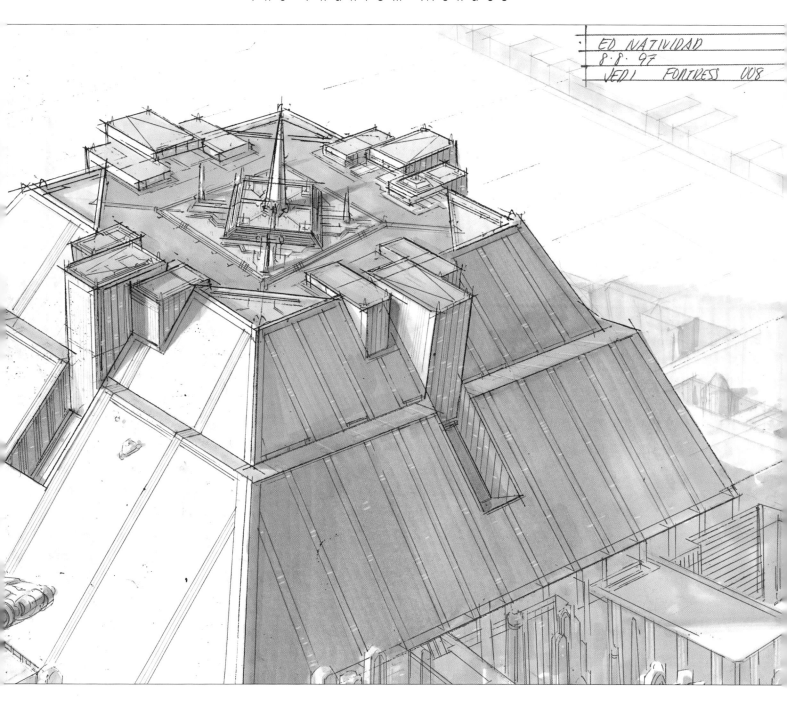

ED NATIVIDAD
8.8.97
JEDI FORTRESS 008

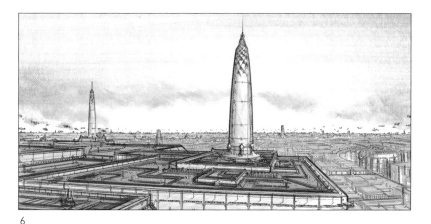

6

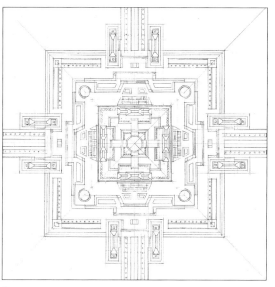

7

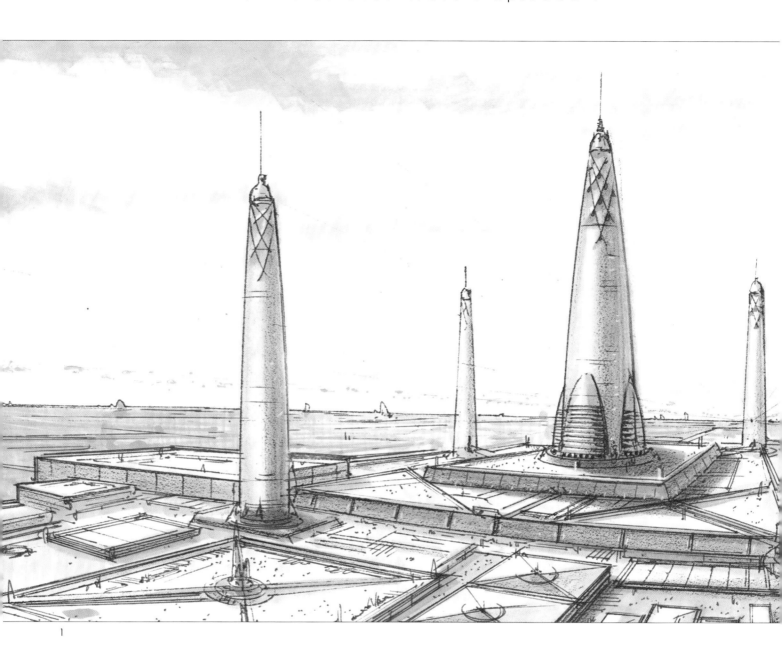

1

Jedi Temple
1, 3–5 Edwin Natividad
2 David Dozoretz
6, 7 Doug Chiang

Animatic frame (2)

In the finished storyboard (1) of the Jedi Temple, the plaza sits atop a pyramid, which stands high above the rest of Coruscant. The Jedi council chamber, in turn, is at the top of the center tower. Inspired by the contrast between the TransAmerica pyramid and the rest of the San Francisco skyline, Chiang and Natividad designed the temple complex to be distinctly different than the rest of Coruscant. The spikes on the roof (3–7) pierce the glass dome and become columns in the interior of the chamber.

2

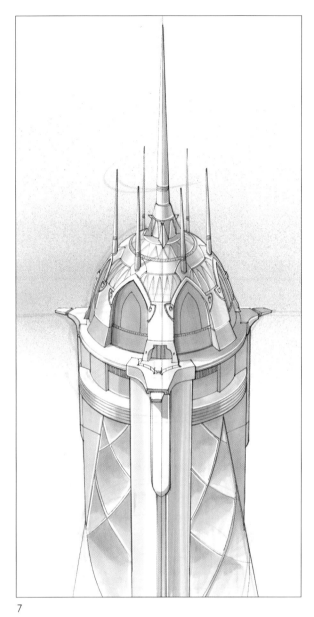

7

3

4

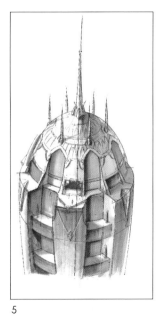

5

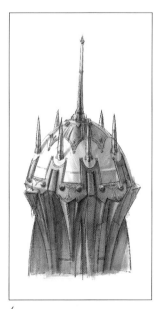

6

1

Jedi Council Chamber, conceptual designs
1 Doug Chiang
2 Edwin Natividad

Since the exterior of the Jedi Temple, with its spikes and spires, was designed first, the interior had to fit within certain constraints. Thus different variations within a certain geometry were tried (1, 2). As for the feel of the room, Lucas had described it as a "gentleman's club, where important people sit in big, comfortable chairs and discuss important matters."

2

3

4

5

6

7

8

Jedi Council Members, conceptual designs
3, 5, 6–8 Iain McCaig
4 Benton Jew

Mace Windu:
Iain McCaig commented, "This initial design [for Mace Windu] is based on ILM modeler Steve Aplin's face; Samuel L. Jackson had yet to be cast (3). The costume is the product of scribbling. People ask how I know when to stop scribbling, and decide a work is finished. I say you have to go too far and destroy it, because then you know when you should have stopped and can go back. If you don't, you leave untold riches out there."

Oppo Rancisis:
Benton Jew based this character (4) on a picture of an old man from a Chinese calendar hanging in his grandparents' house.

Eeth Koth:
McCaig had thought that Eeth Koth, not Mace Windu, would be the leader of the Jedi, and based this portrait on design director Doug Chiang (5).

Yoda:
Since the Jedi were the Republic's law enforcers, McCaig thought it appropriate to dress them in black, like policemen. He also thought it gave the diminutive Yoda a more powerful look (6).

Young Yoda/Yaddle:
This sketch was originally meant to be Yoda as a young child (7). When McCaig drew it he had just read about an eight-year-old Tibetan boy who carried his two-year-old brother twenty-five miles in order to escape the invading Chinese. Feeling that Yoda would have done that, McCaig

gave him a look that conveyed not just youth, but also pain and wisdom. Ultimately, however, this sketch was used to create Yaddle, a female member of Yoda's species.

Ki-Adi-Mundi and alien Jedi:
When Lucas instructed him to create alien Jedi, McCaig took it as an opportunity to draw bizarre parodies of Obi-Wan Kenobi, such as Ki-Adi-Mundi (8), who is Obi-Wan crossed with a whale.

195

1

2

3

4

5

6

7

8

9

Sith Lords, conceptual designs
1–9 Iain McCaig

Before Lucas nailed down the character of Darth Maul, he instructed Iain McCaig to brainstorm what a Sith Lord might look like. At first McCaig gave them large, organic-looking cloaks and bizarre, crusader-influenced helmets (4–6). He also tried a few female versions, for which Lucas instructed him to draw his worst nightmare. The first "Sith Witch" (1) was so terrifying that Lucas asked McCaig to back off a bit and just draw his "second worst nightmare" (2).

Darth Sidious (3), meanwhile, was much simpler. McCaig took the Emperor from *Return of the Jedi*, made him younger, and, for a twist, put him in a white robe instead of a black one.

Simultaneously, McCaig was also creating "evil senators," and began experimenting with facial tattoos and scars (7–9), leading to the creation of Darth Maul. (The senators' likenesses were based on previsualization/effects supervisor David Dozoretz, photographer Greg Gawlowski, and production designer Gavin Bocquet.)

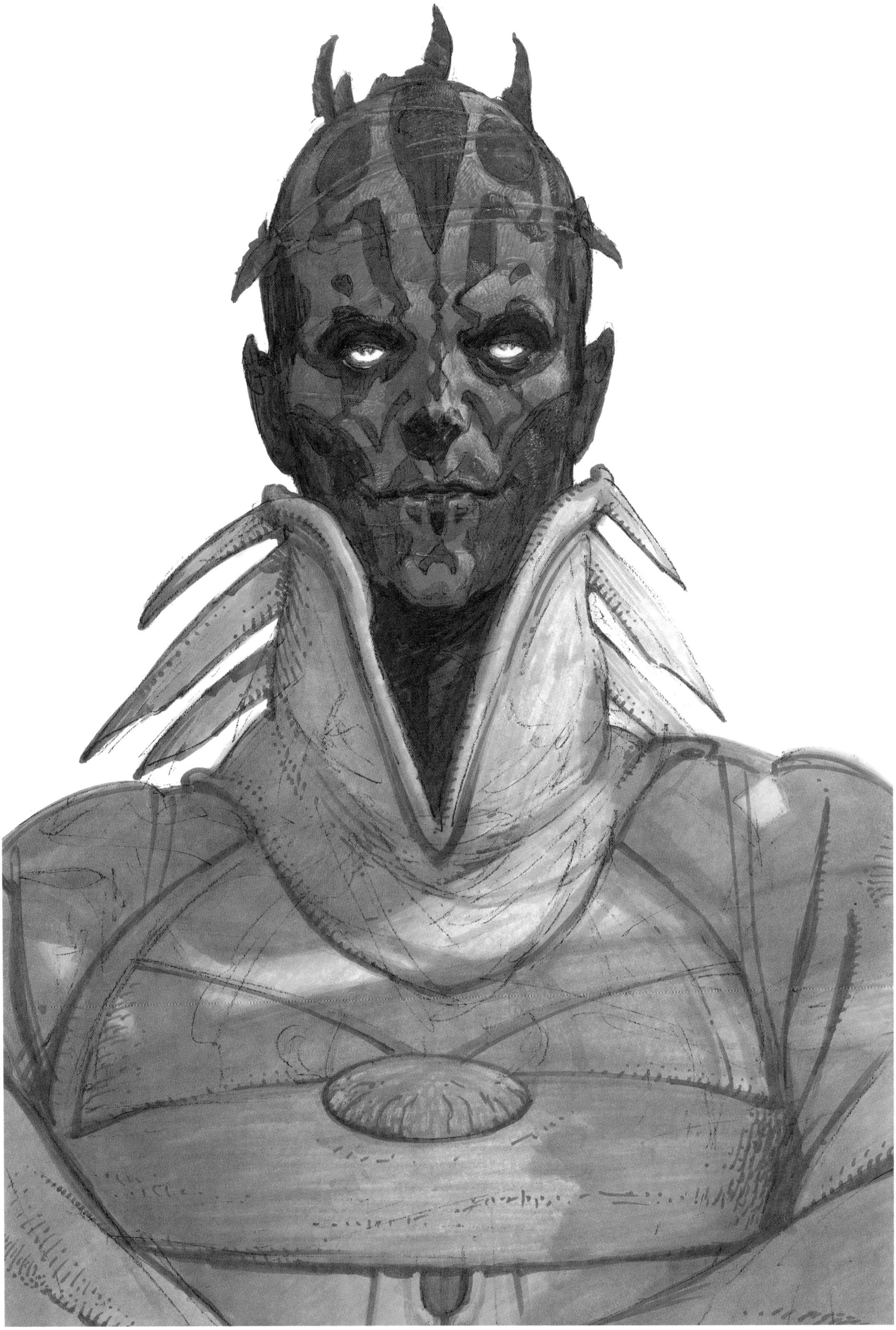

1

2

6

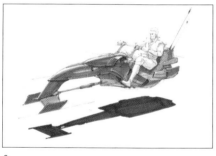

3

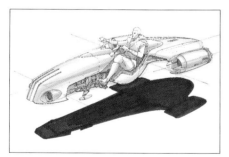

4

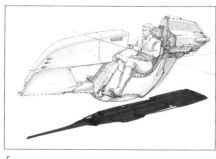

5

Darth Maul, conceptual designs
1, 2 Iain McCaig

The first image of Darth Maul (1) nearly ended up in the trash. McCaig had been dissatisfied with a drawing (based on his own face), and angrily blotted ink all over it. The ink patterns reminded him of the tattoos he had created for the "evil senators," and soon Darth Maul was born. At first the protrusions on top of Maul's head were not horns, but feathers attached by coils of wire which cut into the flesh. These soft feathers, along with the touch of beauty McCaig added to the face, lend an element of seduction to the dark side.

As the details of the Jedi/Sith fights were established, McCaig set to work on a costume in which Darth Maul could spin and kick with ease, and which would flare out dramatically as he moved (2).

Sith speeder, conceptual designs
3–7 Doug Chiang

Chiang started with variations on a hotrod/motorcycle (3). Lucas suggested that Chiang incorporate elements of the droid

7

air bikes (4). However, the longer nose and larger engines made the speeder too heavy. After modifying the nose and engines (5), Chiang and Lucas decided to drop them altogether and make the speeder simpler, lighter, and more compact (7). From there, a finished version was achieved (6), made to resemble a sickle or a scythe: the tools of the "Grim Reaper."

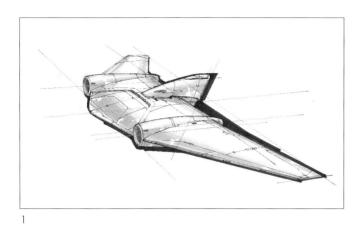

1

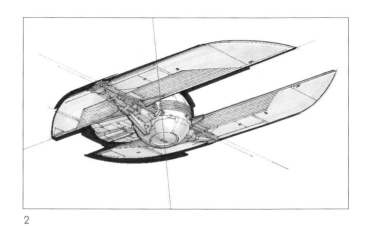

2

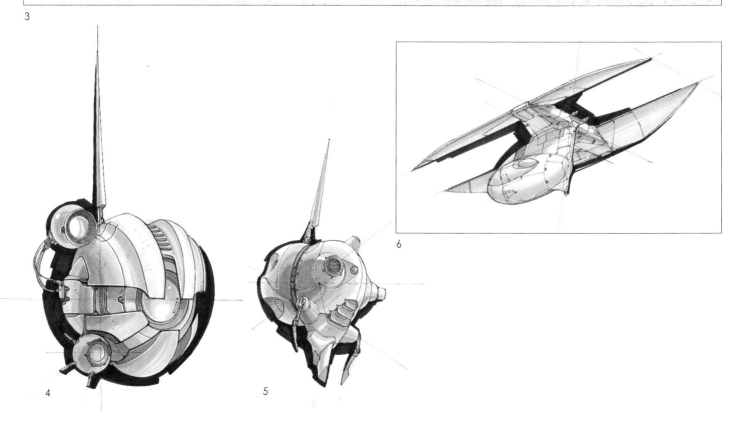

D CHIANG
SITH SHIP RAMP
5-12-97
0873

3

4

5

6

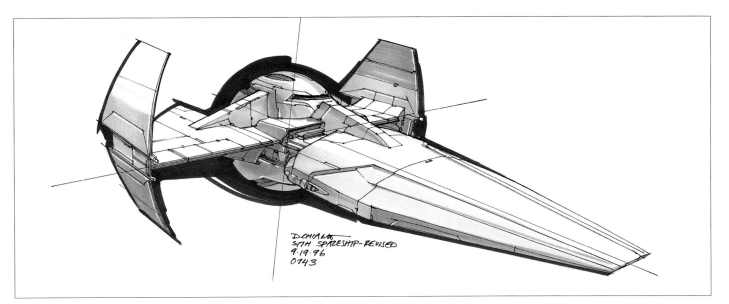

7

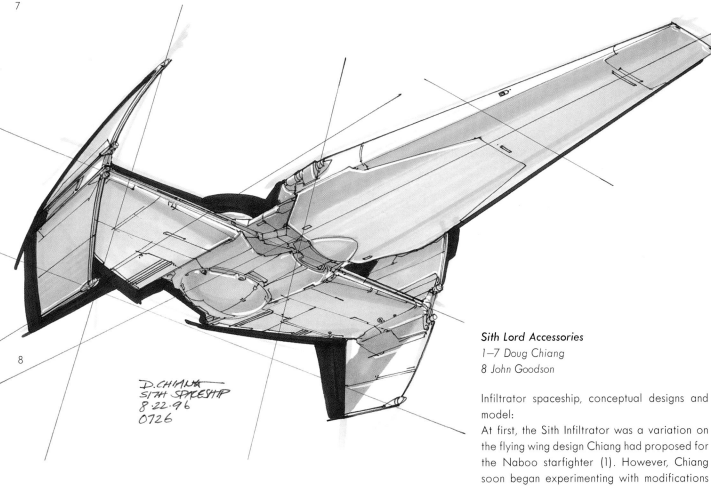

8

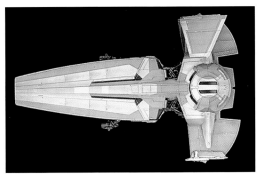

9

Sith Lord Accessories
1–7 Doug Chiang
8 John Goodson

Infiltrator spaceship, conceptual designs and model:

At first, the Sith Infiltrator was a variation on the flying wing design Chiang had proposed for the Naboo starfighter (1). However, Chiang soon began experimenting with modifications of the original trilogy's TIE interceptors (2), even crossing the interceptor with a hang glider (6). Lucas liked these ideas, but asked Chiang to rework them by throwing in a few influences from *Return of the Jedi's Tydirium* shuttle, resulting in the final design (7–9). To allow the ships to land, Chiang designed the Infiltrator with wings that fold up as it touches down. The pilot enters and exits the ball-shaped cockpit via a hatch in the rear (3).

Probe droid, initial and final designs (4, 5).

1

Obi-Wan Kenobi, conceptual designs
1, 4 Iain McCaig
2, 3 Doug Chiang

Early on, Lucas wanted the Jedi design (2) to have a warrior look reminiscent of *Willow*'s Madmartigan. By the second sketch (3), however, Lucas decided on a slightly more peaceful look, including a big, Native American–influenced cloak and a large peace pipe.

When Qui-Gon was introduced, Lucas toyed with the idea of having him be the younger of the two Jedi, and McCaig thus created an older-looking portrait of Obi-Wan (4).

Sith and Jedi costumes (1).

2

3

1

2

3

4

5

Obi-Wan Kenobi and Qui-Gon Jinn
1–3, 6–8 Iain McCaig
4, 5 Kun Chang

6

7

Obi-Wan Kenobi's full-length costume, early (6) and later conceptual designs (1–7)

Obi-Wan as the younger Jedi, conceptual designs:
Before Ewan McGregor was cast, McCaig experimented with different looks for Obi-Wan's face, ranging from smooth to coarse (3, 6).

Qui-Gon Jinn as the younger and elder Jedi, conceptual designs:
McCaig initially drew a young Qui-Gon (2). When Lucas finally decided that Qui-Gon should play the role of mentor, McCaig drew a new portrait (8), based on Liam Neeson.

Jedi lightsabers, conceptual designs (4)

Qui-Gon's hologram projector, conceptual design (5)

Jedi/Sith lightsaber fight, storyboards
Benton Jew
Film frame shot

A big fan of the acrobatic, gravity-defying martial arts battles pioneered by Hong Kong action cinema, Benton Jew worked to imbue the lightsaber fight with a similar energy and vigor. Jew depicts the combat with such ferocity, that his characters often "break frame" (the frame being the rectangular area seen by the camera), indicating that the combatants are almost moving too quickly to follow.

From Sketch to Screen

Jedi Council Chamber
Conceptual design, Doug Chiang
Film set, Gavin Bocquet/UK design team

Queen Amidala's palace dress
Conceptual design, Iain McCaig
Finished costume, Trisha Biggar/costume dept.

Yoda
Conceptual design, Iain McCaig
Finished puppet, Nick Dudman/Chris Barton/creature effects dept.

Droid/Gungan battle
Storyboard, Edwin Natividad
Finished film frame shot, ILM

Throughout the design process, George Lucas brought in members of the production team to consult with the art department. At these meetings, preparations were made for the transition from conceptual design to set construction, both digital and physical. Essentially, Lucas and the production team had to figure out how to take the theories presented by the sketches and models and put them into practice, ultimately committing them to film.

Production designer Gavin Bocquet, with the assistance of supervising art director Peter Russell, was placed in charge of drafting, designing, building, and decorating each and every set. Bocquet was also responsible for scouting locations and modifying them to suit the needs of the production. His knowledge of film stock, lighting, and lenses allowed him to advise all parties as to how a design would appear on film.

Set decorator Peter Walpole oversaw the placement of all the furniture, fixtures, accessories, and trimmings that bring a set to life. This meant that every last piece of junk in Watto's shop, every last curtain in Palpatine's apartment, and every individual flower adorning the walls of Theed had to pass Walpole's inspection.

Costume designer Trisha Biggar worked with concept artist Iain McCaig to turn his fanciful sketches into clothing that could be worn by the appropriate actor, and made certain every costume would look right on camera.

Creature effects supervisor Nick Dudman oversaw the creation of an army of alien costumes, ranging from Rodians and Quarren to the animatronically-controlled puppets such as Yoda and the Neimoidian facemasks. These mechanized creatures were constructed by a team of talented individuals led by animatronic model designer/workshop supervisor Chris Barton. Their work included the construction of elaborate artificial musculature systems made out of wires, springs, and miniature motors, all of which could be operated off-camera by remote control.

Director of photography David Tattersall was responsible for committing the live-action footage to film. He had to determine the overall composition of each scene, a particularly daunting task on a film such as Episode I, since many of the characters and much of the scenery wouldn't even exist until long after the cameras had rolled. Tattersall also had to be consulted on the geography of each scene in order to determine how many cameras should be used, where they should be set up, and what kind of camera moves would be possible. He provided valuable input concerning the color scheme of the sets and costumes, so that he might reconcile factors ranging from lighting to film stock to cameras, lenses, and filters.

Industrial Light & Magic visual effects supervisors John Knoll, Dennis Muren, and Scott Squires worked with animation director Rob Coleman and his team to create all the finished computer animation, and with a group led by model supervisor Steve Gawley to film all the miniature model and motion control camera work. They created nearly everything that didn't directly involve live actors. Their work included generating Jar Jar and the Gungans, the assault on Naboo and droidekas, the Podrace arena and Podrace, the space battle, and the Theed and Coruscant matte paintings. It was their work that transformed the more fantastic designs of the art department into reality and seamlessly integrated them with the live-action footage.

On a film like Episode I, in which every last frame of film is tweaked or touched-up, the line between the art and production teams often blurred. Much of the final look of the film was due to a smooth and creative collaboration between the art department and the members of the production team and their respective staffs. The results speak for themselves.

Art Department

Design Director
Doug Chiang

Production Designer
Gavin Bocquet

Supervising Art Director
Peter Russell

US Concept Artists
Iain McCaig, Terryl Whitlatch, Jay Shuster, Edwin Natividad,
Kurt Kaufman, Marc Gabbana

Storyboard Artist
Benton Jew

Concept Sculptors
Tony McVey, Mark Siegel, Richard Miller, Robert Barnes

Concept Modelmakers
John Goodson, John Duncan, Ellen Lee

Model Set Designer
Bill Beck

US Art Department Coordinators
Jill Jurkowitz, Blake Tucker

US Art Department Assistant
Tom Barratt

Pre-Visualization/Effects Supervisor
David Dozoretz

Pre-Visualization/Effects Artists
Evan Pontoriero, Ryan Tudhope, Kevin Baillie, Jeff Wozniak, Alex Lindsay

Conceptual Researchers
David Craig, Jonathan Bresman, Koichi Kurisu

Set Decorator
Peter Walpole

Costume Designer
Trisha Biggar

Art Directors
Fred Hole, John King, Rod McLean, Phil Harvey

Art Director (Tunisia)
Ben Scott

Draughtsmen
Paul Cross, Neil Morfitt, Gary Tomkins, Toad Tozeur, Julie Philpott,
Jane Clark-Pearce, Philip Elton, Mike Bishop, Lucy Richardson

Scenic Artist
James Gemmill

UK Concept Artists
Tony Wright, Kun Chang

UK Art Department Coordinator
Laura Burrows

Junior Draughtsmen
Helen Xenopoulos, Remo Tozzi

Sculptors
Eddie Butler, Tessa Harrison, Richard Mills, Keith Short, Richard Smith

3-D Computer Modellers
Caine Dickinson, Simon Dunsdon

UK Art Department Assistants
Christopher Challoner, Iain McFadyen, Claire Nia Richards, Emma Tauber

Concept Design Team

DOUG CHIANG—DESIGN DIRECTOR

Doug Chiang studied film at the University of California at Los Angeles, and industrial design at the Center of Creative Studies, College of Art and Design. Chiang got his start as a key animator on the *Pee Wee's Playhouse* television series and soon rose to become a Clio Award–winning commercial director and designer for Rhythm and Hues, Digital Productions, and Robert Abel and Associates. In 1989, Chiang joined Industrial Light & Magic, and, in 1993, became the creative director. During this time, he worked as visual effects art director for such films as *Ghost*, *Back to the Future II*, *The Doors*, *Terminator 2*, *Death Becomes Her*, *Forrest Gump*, *Jumanji*, and *The Mask*. He has earned both an Academy Award and a British Academy Award for *Death Becomes Her* and another British Academy Award for *Forrest Gump*.

As an independent film director, Chiang has received numerous international honors, including First Place in the FOCUS Awards for *Mental Block*. Chiang's personal paintings have appeared nationwide as limited edition prints and posters, as well as in various publications.

GAVIN BOCQUET—PRODUCTION DESIGNER

After studying product design at Newcastle Polytechnic and earning his Master of Design at the Royal College of Art, Gavin Bocquet began his film career as a draughtsman on *The Elephant Man* and *Return of the Jedi*. Rising to the position of assistant art director on *Return to Oz*, *Young Sherlock Holmes*, and *Empire of the Sun*, Bocquet attained the rank of art director on *Dangerous Liaisons*, and served on *Eric the Viking* and *Cry Freedom* in the same capacity. On *Cry Freedom* he had the good luck to work alongside Stuart Craig who, along with Norman Reynolds, are the men he regards as his mentors.

Bocquet's credits as production designer range from the British television series *Yellowthread Street* and the U.S. television series *The Young Indiana Jones Chronicles*, for which he received one Emmy award and two nominations, to the feature films *Kafka*, *Radioland Murders*, and the upcoming *Rocky and Bullwinkle*.

PETER RUSSELL—SUPERVISING ART DIRECTOR

Starting his career as a teacher of both art and physical education, Peter Russell spent his spare time striving to break into film. After two years of trying, he was hired by the legendary designer Stuart Craig to work as an art department assistant on *Saturn III*, and it was there that Russell first met Gavin Bocquet. After serving in the same capacity on *Flash Gordon*, he became a junior draughtsman on *The French Lieutenant's Woman*, and rose to the position of assistant art director on *The Professionals*. He became an art director on *A Night on the Town*, and served in that capacity in films ranging from *Aliens* to *The Borrowers* to *White Squall*, as well as on *The Mummy* and the upcoming *Gladiator*. Russell considers Norman Dorme, John Box, Stuart Craig, and the late Anton Furst to be his role models, and endeavors to match their high degree of excellence. His credits also include *Never Say Never Again*, *Indiana Jones and the Temple of Doom*, *A Passage to India*, *Who Framed Roger Rabbit*, *Indiana Jones and the Last Crusade*, *Batman*, *Judge Dredd*, and *The Saint*.

IAIN McCAIG
CONCEPT ARTIST

A filmmaker and artist, Iain McCaig has worked on concept designs for both *The Phantom Menace* and *Star Wars: Episode II*, as well as the Special Edition of *Return of the Jedi*.

Recently he served as character art director on Industrial Light & Magic's first all-digital feature film, *Frankenstein*, as well as conceptual designer on Francis Ford Coppola's *Pinocchio*. He has storyboarded many films, including *Terminator 2*, *Hook*, and *Interview with the Vampire*.

In March of 1998, McCaig's first foray into the world of directing, *The Face*, debuted at the Santa Barbara Film Festival and won the Houston International Film Festival's Gold Medal for Best Family Film.

McCaig is also a widely published illustrator. His work includes book and record covers, limited edition prints, posters, advertising, and children's books.

TERRYL WHITLATCH
CONCEPT ARTIST

Originally a zoology student at Sonoma State University, Terryl Whitlatch finished her college career at the Academy of Art College in San Francisco. While still a student, Whitlatch was hired by LucasArts to create alien creatures for the game The Dig. In 1994 she was recruited by the *Jumanji* team at Industrial Light & Magic. Her credits also include *The Indian in the Cupboard*, *Dragonheart*, *Men in Black*, and Budweiser and Honeycomb commercials as well as the *Star Wars Trilogy Special Edition*. Whitlatch joined the Episode I crew in January of 1995 to lend her expertise in creature design and animation. From time to time she works as an illustrator for Lucas Publishing, and she has also created animal-themed merchandise for Willitz Designs and the World Wildlife Fund. Whitlatch is currently doing pre-production design for Disney animation.

JAY SHUSTER
CONCEPT ARTIST

Born in Pontiac, Michigan to a family of designers, Jay Shuster grew up surrounded by the manufacturers of America's most popular icon: the automobile.

An artist and modelmaker almost since infancy, Shuster saw *Star Wars* when he was six and realized right then what he was going to do with his life. Shuster thus spent the next twelve years in his parents' basement, honing his design skills by transforming model car kits into spaceships and making short films.

After studying industrial design at Detroit's Center for Creative Studies College of Art Design, Shuster worked briefly as a designer for various multi-media and video game companies. He moved on to freelance work as a storyboard artist for ILM's commercial division, all the while aspiring to join the *Star Wars* art department. According to Shuster, this aspiration "turned to perspiration" when he was invited to make the move to Skywalker Ranch. What ensued were four years of concentrated creative mayhem and a convergence of Shuster's diverse skills into the ultimate realization of a childhood dream.

EDWIN NATIVIDAD
CONCEPT ARTIST

Edwin Natividad attended art school in Detroit, where he double majored in transportation design and illustration, but also focused heavily on human anatomy. He interned at the Ford Motor Company and later was given the opportunity to work at General Motors' advanced concept center in Thousand Oaks, California. Returning for his senior year of college in 1990, Natividad was eventually suspended for taking liberties with the curriculum. He then journeyed back to California with no job and no clue, but lots of time to see and explore the southwest.

Since joining ILM in 1994, Natividad has worked on *Forrest Gump*, *Casper*, *Jumanji*, and *Spawn*. While in Los Angeles, he worked on *Batman and Robin*, *Armageddon* and *Star Trek: Insurrection*. He also teaches occasionally at Art Center College of Design in Pasadena. After *Star Wars*, he plans to move to Hawaii, go fishing, and live like Paul Gauguin.

KURT KAUFMAN
CONCEPT ARTIST

The son of a Ford automobile designer and a fan of the futuristic art of Syd Mead, Kurt Kaufman found *Star Wars* to be not only a stunning movie but also a creative awakening that influenced his artistic outlook from then on. After graduating from the Art Center College of Design's transportation design department, Kaufman worked on future concept illustration for Lockheed. From there, he moved on to film and theme park work, as well as commercial illustration, and from time to time taught at the Art Center College of Design before moving to Marin to work for Industrial Light & Magic. His film credits include *Hook*, *Death Becomes Her*, *Jurassic Park*, and various commercials. He has also served as an art director at 3DO and has done computer illustration and Alias work for such clients as Apple, Mattel, Gingko Design, and Electronic Arts.

BENTON JEW
STORYBOARD ARTIST

In 1988, while still a student at the Academy of Art College and the University of San Francisco, Benton Jew was hired by Industrial Light & Magic. Subsequent to earning a BFA, he continued working for the ILM art department, cranking out copious amounts of concept and storyboard work for feature films, commercials, and attractions, working his way up to becoming visual effects art director for *The Mask*. Before joining ILM, Jew's freelance clients included the architectural firm Holt, Hinshaw, Pfau, and Jones; Galoob Toys; the Oakland Athletics; and *Sacramento Magazine*. His film credits include *The Mummy*, *Men in Black*, *Dragonheart*, *John Carpenter's Village of the Damned*, and *Jurassic Park*.

TONY McVEY
CONCEPT SCULPTOR

Tony McVey began his career creating dioramas for the British Museum's natural history division, before moving on to work as a sculptor and designer on Jim Henson's *The Dark Crystal*. After that, more film work quickly followed, from the aliens of *Return of the Jedi* to the Mogwai of *Gremlins*. As McVey continued to work in film, he picked up skills as a puppeteer and stop-motion animator while working on *Star Trek II*, *Enemy Mine*, *Howard the Duck*, and *The Ewok Adventure*. He soon started his own commercial production company, working for such clients as Swatch, Prudential, and Molsen Ale as a designer, director, and effects supervisor. His current company, Menagerie Productions, has done design and concept work for clients ranging from Disney to Amblin to NBC to Time Warner.

ROBERT BARNES
CONCEPT SCULPTOR

Much of Robert Barnes' childhood was spent competing with his older brother to create the ultimate monster. Accordingly, his first major project was to draw enough creatures to obscure his bedroom's Humpty-Dumpty wallpaper.

Countless creatures later, Barnes was studying physics in college and working as an audio engineer when he decided to focus his energy on becoming a "serious" artist. After studying sculpture and design at Sonoma State University and Art Center College of Design, Barnes settled in to pursue a degree from the industrial design program at California State University, Long Beach.

Barnes got a thorough initiation to film production as an intern in the ILM art department, working on *Casper*, *Jumanji*, *Star Trek VII*, and several commercial productions. Upon graduation from CSULB, Barnes returned to the ILM art department as production assistant. He was soon recruited by Doug Chiang to join the *Star Wars* team, calling upon his skills for building vehicle and set models, storyboarding, digital imaging, and painting and sculpting creature designs. Barnes' drawings can also be seen on an array of Episode I products, which may or may not include children's wallpaper.

JOHN GOODSON
CONCEPT MODELMAKER

John Goodson has always been fascinated by miniatures and special effects. Growing up with a father in the Air Force gave him an exposure to a wide variety of aircraft and hardware. Seeing *Star Wars* gave him a focus. Goodson avidly studied the artist biographies in the original *Art of Star Wars* books, hoping to duplicate their educational paths so that he too might one day work in film. Although he achieved his objective, he still finds it hard to believe.

At North Carolina State School of Design, Goodson studied product design and took a variety of jobs geared toward his goal of joining the effects industry. These included architectural and product appearance modeling, exhibit design, automotive body shop, set and prop construction, and prototype engineering.

Goodson joined ILM in 1988, and has served as chief modelmaker, model project supervisor, art director, and concept modeler. He is currently a designer. His credits include *Deep Impact*, *The Rocketeer*, *Star Trek VI-VIII*, *Back to the Future II*, *Batman Returns*, *The Abyss*, *Ghostbusters II*, *The Star Wars Trilogy Special Edition*, and EPCOT's "Body Wars" ride.

JOHN DUNCAN
CONCEPT MODELMAKER

John Duncan has been hooked on special effects all his life and considers the idea that a small model can look as big as an aircraft carrier to be the greatest magic trick in the world. John Duncan built his first model kit when he was six years old. It was a World War II submarine and because he was too young to use regular model glue, he used Elmer's glue, which quickly dissolved in the bathtub.

His work has improved since then.

Undeterred, Duncan pursued his dream of being an effects artist in school, hoping but never imagining he'd work for the illustrious Industrial Light & Magic. After graduating from Northern Arizona University with a degree in Film Production, he went on to make music videos and worked as a technical director for an NBC affiliate's evening news program. His first job at Industrial Light & Magic was building models for the Acura "Hot Wheels" commercial. He has since gone on to work on such films as *Star Trek: First Contact*, *Independence Day*, *Men in Black*, *Broken Arrow*, *Starship Troopers*, *Con Air*, and *The Truman Show*.

ELLEN LEE
CONCEPT MODELMAKER

Ellen Lee's childhood fascination with all things creative and technical led her to study three-dimensional design at Stanford University's mechanical engineering school. After graduating, she went on to work in Berlin, Germany, as a mechanical engineering assistant, and, later, in Seoul, Korea, designing for Daewoo Electronics. On her return to the U.S., she pursued a Master of Industrial Design degree in New York City. There she furthered her skills in drawing, model construction, studio photography, and computer graphics (CADD & Alias).

While still in school, Lee interned at Lucasfilm, where she met the renowned Doug Chiang. A few months later, he invited her to join the *Star Wars* art department. Thus, she began work as concept modelmaker for Episode I, her first feature film.

In addition to her pre-visualization work for the *Star Wars* art department, Lee has also worked for Lucasfilm art directing and designing various graphics for print, film, and television, as well as exhibits for the release of Episode I.

She is also the designer of this book.

DAVID DOZORETZ
PRE-VISUALIZATION/EFFECTS
SUPERVISOR

David Dozoretz joined ILM in 1992 as an art production intern. Upon completing his internship, he was asked to return the following summer as a production assistant. Dozoretz soon became an art director assistant, and helped launch the production of 3D digital concept art and animatics. His *Mission: Impossible* work impressed Rick McCallum enough to invite Dozoretz to lead the Episode I pre-visualization/effects team. From mid-1995 to mid-1999, the team designed over 1800 shots for *The Phantom Menace*, and completed the final visual effects for over 100 shots.

Dozoretz recently worked with San Francisco–based Combustion Studios to design a futuristic computer simulation ride opening in Tokyo, Japan, in early 2000.

At the University of Arizona, Dozoretz wrote, produced, and directed many student films and helped establish the University's first digital multimedia lab. His credits include *The Star Wars Trilogy Special Edition*, *Dragonheart*, *Casper*, *Disclosure*, *Star Trek: Generations*, *Forrest Gump*, and numerous commercial and music video projects.

Dozoretz has lectured worldwide on the application of digital technologies to the filmmaking process.

EVAN PONTORIERO
PRE-VISUALIZATION/EFFECTS ARTIST

As an undergraduate at the University of Maryland, Evan Pontoriero studied sculpture, lithography, and graphic design. Upon graduating, he worked as a graphic designer and animator for several multimedia and CD-ROM development companies. While creating 3D animation and designs for the CD-ROM title Battle of the Ironclads, Evan had the opportunity to work with *New Hope* concept artist Ron Cobb.

Before joining the *Star Wars* art department Evan founded his own 3D design studio, where he acted as design director on Bungie Software's real-time 3D game Weekend Warrior, the first game to utilize Apple's QuickDraw 3D technology. He also worked for several years creating graphics and animation for broadcast and video. After serving on Episode I, Evan transferred to Industrial Light & Magic to work on the upcoming 3D animated *Frankenstein* feature.

ALEX LINDSAY
PRE-VISUALIZATION/EFFECTS ARTIST

After leaving careers in radio and acting, Lindsay began his graphics career in print as a graphic designer for Prime Sports Network. Later he worked in broadcast design and as a creative director for Anark's Galapagos game. Lindsay has been a featured speaker and writer for a variety of conferences and magazines, and teaches animation concepts at San Francisco State University. He has also produced visual tools for animators and artists, including the CD-ROM Surface of Reality. Episode I is his first feature film.

KEVIN A. BAILLIE
PRE-VISUALIZATION/EFFECTS ARTIST

While attending Shorecrest High School in Seattle, Washington, Baillie, a specialist in two- and three-dimensional computer art and animation, worked with companies such as Microsoft and the Space Needle Corporation. Along with partner Ryan Tudhope, he also formed Aura Studios, a visual effects company that interacted with Shorecrest High School and Trionix Corporation to develop 3D content for entertainment and architectural visualization purposes.

While employed by Microsoft to develop 3D animation for product research and marketing purposes, Baillie was sought out and interviewed by the George Lucas Educational Foundation for their then-upcoming documentary, *Learn & Live*. Through this documentary Baillie was offered a position with Lucasfilm's specialized group of computer artists shortly after his high school graduation in July of 1997. Within a short period of time, Baillie became an integral part of Lucas' pre-visualization team, assisting in the process of designing hundreds of visual effects shots for Episode I.

RYAN TUDHOPE
PRE-VISUALIZATION/EFFECTS ARTIST

Ryan Tudhope took an after-school interest in computer graphics and parlayed it into a job at Skywalker Ranch by the age of 18. Tudhope joined Microsoft's Graphics & Multimedia division in early 1996, where he was contracted to design and produce short animations for the purpose of demonstrating and marketing new technology. Shortly thereafter, Tudhope co-founded Aura Studios with colleague Kevin Baillie, a partnership specializing in digital media and three-dimensional animation.

While attending Shorecrest High School in Seattle, Washington, the George Lucas Educational Foundation's flagship documentary *Learn & Live* scouted Tudhope for his School to Career work within the industry. After seeing his computer graphics reel, both Rick McCallum and George Lucas gave Tudhope the incredible opportunity to join the *Star Wars* art department.

JEFF WOZNIAK
PRE-VISUALIZATION/EFFECTS ARTIST

Originally from Minneapolis, Minnesota, Jeff studied economics and communications at Stanford University. While there, he pursued a long-standing interest in film and, in particular, the principles of motion picture sound. Jeff eventually parlayed this interest into a job with Lucasfilm's THX Division. During the four years he worked for the THX Theatre Alignment Program (TAP), he helped to ensure that films such as *The Lion King*, *The Star Wars Trilogy Special Edition*, *Men in Black*, and *Titanic*, were seen and heard by audiences as the filmmakers intended.

While still passionate about motion picture presentation, Wozniak found himself gravitating toward film production, and in early 1996, began to pursue a burgeoning interest in computer graphics. After more than two years of experimenting with various graphics software packages at home, Jeff submitted a demo reel of his work to Lucasfilm, and ultimately joined the *Star Wars* animatics team in April of 1998.

BLAKE TUCKER
ART DEPT. COORDINATOR

Blake Tucker hails from a variety of places, among them New Hampshire, Stanford University, and the Lucasfilm archives. He has extensive experience in music composition and technology, computers, film production, and gourmet cooking. He got his start at Lucasfilm in the licensing department, working on the first *Star Wars* Summit in 1994. When not trying to be a jack of all trades, Tucker functions as the production coordinator in the *Star Wars* art department, but even there he likes to change his hats. He added the Huttese subtitles to Episode I, contributes his computer graphics and layout skills as needed, and sometimes will even function as an on-site technical support representative. During his affiliation with the Lucasfilm archives, Tucker worked on costume/character appearances for *The Star Wars Trilogy Special Edition*, the CD-ROM game Rebel Assault II, *The Oprah Winfrey Show*, and a *Star Wars* Taco Bell commercial. He has also been known to appear in costume as an Imperial Officer.

BILL BECK
MODEL SET DESIGNER

After graduating from Hamline University with a Bachelor of Arts degree, Bill Beck went on to receive Masters degrees in both Art and Architecture from the University of Califonia at Berkeley. Starting his career as an art instructor at Berkeley, Beck soon joined the Rawson Drug and Sundry company as a graphic artist. After two years there, he left to work in film, television, and theater, where he specialized in set, prop, lighting, and effects design, serving on such productions as *Play It Again Sam*, *Streets of San Francisco* and *Crime of the Century*.

In 1979, Beck joined ILM, working on such films as *The Empire Strikes Back*, *Raiders of the Lost Ark*, and *Star Trek II: The Wrath of Khan* in a variety of capacities, including modelmaker, special effects technician, carpenter, draughtsman, and manager of the wood shop. He soon thereafter became a set designer, lending his talents to *Back to the Future II*, *Indiana Jones and the Last Crusade*, *James and the Giant Peach*, *Jack*, and *Sphere*, to name a few. He is currently working on the forthcoming all-digital version of *Frankenstein*.

JONATHAN BRESMAN
CONCEPTUAL RESEARCHER

While an undergraduate at Harvard, Jonathan Bresman spent his summers working on *The Young Indiana Jones Chronicles*, *Radioland Murders*, and *Star Wars: Episode I The Phantom Menace*. During his senior year, he was asked to continue working on Episode I as a conceptual researcher, and he gladly converted his dorm room into the East Coast outpost of the Lucasfilm empire. Upon graduating in 1996, Bresman returned to Skywalker Ranch. Once principal photography began, he joined the *Star Wars* documentary crew as www.starwars.com's production correspondent, chronicling the filming of Episode I in England, Italy, and Tunisia.

A former student of Spike Lee and Jamaica Kincaid, Bresman has also studied animation writing at the American Film Institute's Television Writers Workshop. He has interned for Marvel and Valiant Comics, as well as for *MAD* magazine, for whom he has worked as a freelance writer. Prior to coming to Lucasfilm, Bresman served as a research intern at *The Late Show with David Letterman*.

He is also the author of this book.

DAVID CRAIG
CONCEPTUAL RESEARCHER

David Craig has played various roles in the creation of film and theater works—designer, director, writer, production researcher, and creative consultant. Even before graduating from the University of California, Santa Cruz, with a degree in theater and medieval history, David began experimenting with telling stories using new technology and traditional techniques—combinations of actors, marionettes, other nonhuman actors, music, and sound recordings. His experience also includes advertising, marketing, and corporate identity projects focused on entertainment media.

His work for Lucasfilm Ltd. runs the gamut from *Return of the Jedi* to *Tucker* and *Mishima*, from *Willow* to *The Young Indiana Jones Chronicles*, and from curating the Lucasfilm archive to brainstorming with the *Phantom Menace* art department. Other film production and marketing projects in which he has participated include *Blade Runner*, *Barry Lyndon*, *Under Fire*, *The Outlaw—Josey Wales*, *King Kong*, *Hammett*, *The Land Before Time*, *Little Treasure*, and an array of documentaries.

Acknowledgments

Recognition and thanks must be extended to the many behind-the-scenes people who facilitated the creation of the vast body of concept work. Without their help, Episode I could not have happened.

First and foremost, praise and gratitude must be heaped upon David Craig, our veteran conceptual consultant and researcher. His encyclopedic knowledge of anthropology, archaeology, astronomy, film, sociology, world history, and martial arts informed our every design and greatly improved the look of the film. His weekly visits to the art department always prompted lively discussions of art, politics, science, philosophy, and religion, and reminded us that creation can only take place when the mind is active. He taught us that true art cannot be created in a vacuum, and helped each of us to become a bit more of a Renaissance man.

We must also thank Jo Donaldson, Cheryl Edwards, Jenny Craik, Janet Silk, Paloma Anoveros, Halina Krukowski, and Pooneh Zandazma, our dedicated library staff, as well as Jon Bresman and Koichi Kurisu, our junior conceptual researchers. If David Craig was our teacher, then they were our after-school tutors, helping us with our research "homework" day in and day out, one assignment at a time. Without their assistance, we could never have navigated Lucasfilm's vast research archive, and our work wouldn't have had the grounding in the real world that George Lucas demands.

Greg Gawlowski, our photographer, Roel Robles, our art department assistant, and Tina Mills and Scott Carter, our image coordinators, helped us to catalog the thousands of pieces of artwork generated over four years. We would have been unable to guide the evolution of this film without being able to compare and contrast and ultimately alter the many different versions of our designs without the immense database that they built for us.

When we were faced with a storyboarding crunch, John Bell, Erich Rigling, Peter Chan, Chuck Pyle, Tom Watson, and Paul Topolos jumped in on short notice to help us furiously pencil away and meet our deadline. Emmanuel Shiu, Euisung Lee and Kory Jones did the same for us on the animatic front, and Greg Smith lent a hand with the sculpting. We would also like to thank Apple Computer for their technical assistance.

Every one of the people mentioned above had a direct impact on the look of Episode I, and even though some of them never actually put pencil to paper in a literal sense, they all helped to generate much of the artwork seen in this volume. We wish to thank them for their invaluable assistance and their tireless work.

D.CHIANG

Doug Chiang
Skywalker Ranch
May 1999

From Movie to Marketing

EPISODE I

1

STAR WARS EPISODE I

2

Movie posters
1, 2 Teaser (November 1998)
3 One-sheet (March 1999)

George Lucas—art director (1–3), concept designer (3)
Jim Ward—marketing director (1–3)
Doug Chiang—art director (3)
Ellen Lee—concept designer (1), graphic designer (1–3)
Drew Struzan—illustrator (3)

As the film entered the post-production phase, Doug Chiang and Ellen Lee teamed up with Lucasfilm director of marketing Jim Ward and veteran poster artist Drew Struzan to launch a poster campaign that would carry on the *Star Wars* tradition. While Chiang and Struzan worked to create a traditional, painted poster, Lee used digital technology to create photorealistic "paintings" of her own.

Under Jim Ward's supervision, Chiang, Lee, and Struzan were able to distill Lucas' universe into a handful of tight, focused images that could act as symbols for the film, and let audiences worldwide know that Lucas hadn't forgotten them.

3

Ellen Lee, Rick McCallum, Jonathan Bresman, and George Lucas after a *Star Wars* art deparment meeting at Skywalker Ranch

About the Author

While an undergraduate at Harvard, Jonathan Bresman spent his summers working on *The Young Indiana Jones Chronicles*, *Radioland Murders*, and *Star Wars*: Episode I *The Phantom Menace*. During his senior year, he was promoted to conceptual researcher, and telecommuted from his dorm room. After graduating, Bresman returned to Lucasfilm. Once principal photography began, he followed along with the *Star Wars* documentary crew and as www.starwars.com's production correspondent. A former student of Spike Lee and Jamaica Kincaid, Bresman has also studied animation writing at AFI's Television Writers Workshop. He has interned for Marvel and Valiant Comics, as well as for *MAD* magazine, for whom he has worked as a freelance writer. Prior to coming to Lucasfilm, Bresman served as a research intern at *The Late Show with David Letterman*. He resides in Berkeley, CA.

About the Designer

Ellen Lee, conceptual modelmaker for the *Star Wars* art department, has been an active paricipant in *Star Wars*: Episode I *The Phantom Menace* from pre-production through the making of this book. A graduate of Stanford University's Product Design Program, she began her work at Lucasfilm in 1995 after working abroad and pursuing Masters work in industrial design. She has worked with George Lucas and Lucasfilm marketing director Jim Ward to create the film's logo and the teaser poster featuring Anakin Skywalker and the shadow of Darth Vader.